How to start a dog walking business

Introduction to the Dog Walking Business

Welcome to the world of dog walking, a rewarding and dynamic industry that blends the love of animals with the independence and excitement of running your own business. Whether you are an experienced dog lover or someone looking to break free from the 9-to-5 grind, starting a dog walking business offers a unique opportunity to create a fulfilling career while providing a valuable service to pet owners in your community.

In recent years, the demand for professional dog walking services has soared. With more people working long hours or traveling frequently, the need for reliable, trustworthy individuals to care for their beloved pets has never been greater. This growing trend presents a lucrative market for aspiring dog walkers, with potential for steady income and business growth.

This book, "How to Start a Dog Walking Business," is designed to guide you through every step of establishing your own successful dog walking venture. From the initial stages of research and planning to the intricacies of daily operations and client management, we will cover all the essential aspects needed to launch and sustain a thriving business.

In the following chapters, you will learn how to:

- Conduct thorough market research to understand your target audience and competition.
- Develop a comprehensive business plan that outlines your goals, strategies, and financial projections.

- Navigate the legal requirements and obtain the necessary permits and insurance.
- Create a strong brand identity that sets you apart from competitors.
- Effectively market your services and build a loyal client base.
- Manage your finances, schedule, and employees to ensure smooth operations.
- Provide top-notch care for the dogs under your watch, ensuring their safety and well-being.

By the end of this book, you will have the knowledge and confidence to start your own dog walking business, equipped with practical advice, expert tips, and real-life examples from successful entrepreneurs in the industry. Whether you aim to run a solo operation or expand into a larger company with multiple employees, the insights provided here will help you achieve your business goals.

So, let's embark on this journey together. Get ready to turn your passion for dogs into a profitable and enjoyable career, making a positive impact on the lives of pets and their owners alike. Welcome to the exciting world of dog walking!

Copyright © 2024

All rights reserved. No part of this book may be reproduced in any form or by any electronic or mechanical means, including information storage and retrieval systems, without permission in writing from the publisher, except by a reviewer, who may quote brief passages in a review.

The information contained in this book is for general information purposes only. The information is provided by naciro and while we endeavor to keep the information up to date and correct, we make no representations or warranties of any kind, express or implied, about the completeness, accuracy, reliability, suitability or availability with respect to the book or the information, products, services, or related graphics contained in the book for any purpose. Any reliance you place on such information is therefore strictly at your own risk.

All trademarks and registered trademarks are the property of their respective owners and are used in this book only for identification and explanation.

Permission to use copyrighted material in this book should be obtained from the copyright owner or the publisher.

This book is not intended to provide medical, legal, or financial advice, and the author and publisher specifically disclaim any liability for any loss or damage caused or alleged to be caused directly or indirectly by the information in this book.

Naciro and the publisher of this book do not endorse or recommend any commercial products, processes, or services. The views and opinions of authors expressed in this book do not necessarily state or reflect those of the publisher of this book.

Contents

Chapter 1: Introduction to Dog Walking Business

- Overview of the dog walking industry
- Benefits of starting a dog walking business
- Understanding the demand for dog walking services

Chapter 2: Research and Planning

- Conducting market research
- Identifying your target market
- Analyzing your competition
- Setting business goals

Chapter 3: Developing a Business Plan

- Components of a solid business plan
- Financial planning and budgeting
- Setting short-term and long-term goals

Chapter 4: Legal Requirements and Permits

- Understanding local regulations
- Registering your business
- Obtaining necessary permits and licenses

Chapter 5: Choosing a Business Structure

- Sole proprietorship vs. LLC vs. corporation
- Pros and cons of each structure
- Choosing the right structure for your business

Chapter 6: Setting Up Your Business

- Finding a suitable location (if applicable)

- Setting up a home office
- Organizing your workspace

Chapter 7: Insurance and Liability

- Importance of insurance for a dog walking business
- Types of insurance coverage needed
- Finding the right insurance provider

Chapter 8: Creating a Brand Identity

- Choosing a business name
- Designing a logo
- Creating a brand message and mission statement

Chapter 9: Pricing Your Services

- Determining your pricing strategy
- Researching market rates
- Creating pricing packages

Chapter 10: Marketing Your Dog Walking Business

- Developing a marketing plan
- Utilizing social media
- Creating a professional website

Chapter 11: Networking and Building Relationships

- Joining local business groups and associations
- Partnering with pet stores and vets
- Building a client referral program

Chapter 12: Creating Contracts and Agreements

- Importance of written agreements
- Key components of a dog walking contract

- Managing client expectations

Chapter 13: Managing Finances

- Setting up a business bank account
- Tracking income and expenses
- Understanding taxes and deductions

Chapter 14: Scheduling and Time Management

- Creating an efficient schedule
- Managing multiple clients
- Utilizing scheduling software

Chapter 15: Hiring Employees or Contractors

- Deciding when to hire help
- Finding and interviewing candidates
- Training and managing employees

Chapter 16: Ensuring Dog Safety

- Basic dog handling skills
- Understanding dog behavior
- Dealing with emergencies

Chapter 17: Providing Excellent Customer Service

- Communicating effectively with clients
- Handling complaints and issues
- Going above and beyond for client satisfaction

Chapter 18: Growing Your Business

- Expanding your service area
- Offering additional services (pet sitting, training)
- Scaling your business

Chapter 19: Utilizing Technology

- Software and apps for dog walkers
- GPS tracking for client peace of mind
- Managing bookings and payments online

Chapter 20: Social Media and Online Presence

- Creating engaging content
- Building a following on social media
- Utilizing online reviews and testimonials

Chapter 21: Handling Difficult Dogs and Situations

- Techniques for handling aggressive dogs
- Managing multiple dogs at once
- Dealing with unforeseen circumstances

Chapter 22: Health and Wellness for Dogs

- Understanding basic canine health
- Recognizing signs of illness or injury
- Providing first aid for dogs

Chapter 23: Legal Considerations and Liability

- Understanding liability issues
- Protecting yourself legally
- Keeping detailed records

Chapter 24: Client Retention Strategies

- Building long-term relationships with clients
- Rewarding loyal clients
- Consistently providing high-quality service

Chapter 25: Seasonal Considerations

- Adjusting your services for different seasons
- Handling extreme weather conditions
- Keeping dogs safe in varying climates

Chapter 26: Self-Care and Avoiding Burnout

- Managing your physical health
- Finding work-life balance
- Avoiding burnout in a physically demanding job

Chapter 27: Continuing Education and Certification

- Importance of ongoing learning
- Certification programs for dog walkers
- Staying updated on industry trends

Chapter 28: Case Studies and Success Stories

- Learning from successful dog walking businesses
- Real-life examples and tips
- Applying their strategies to your business

Chapter 29: Handling Business Challenges

- Common challenges in the dog walking industry
- Problem-solving techniques
- Staying motivated during tough times

Chapter 30: Future Trends in the Dog Walking Industry

- Emerging trends and technologies
- Adapting to changes in the market
- Planning for the future of your business

Chapter 1: Introduction to the Dog Walking Business

Overview of the Dog Walking Industry

Welcome to the vibrant world of dog walking, where passion for pets meets entrepreneurial spirit. The dog walking industry has experienced remarkable growth in recent years, driven by changes in lifestyle and an increasing awareness of pet well-being. As more people juggle busy schedules, long work hours, or frequent travel, the need for reliable and professional dog walking services has never been greater.

Evolution and Growth: What was once seen as a casual favor among neighbors or a hobby for dog enthusiasts has transformed into a thriving business sector. Today, professional dog walkers play a crucial role in the lives of pet owners by providing essential care and companionship to their beloved dogs. This evolution is not just about walking dogs; it's about ensuring they receive the exercise, socialization, and mental stimulation they need to thrive.

Diverse Clientele: The clientele of dog walking businesses spans across various demographics. From busy professionals in urban areas to elderly pet owners who may find it challenging to exercise their pets adequately, there is a wide range of potential clients seeking these services. Each client has unique needs and expectations, making it essential for dog walkers to tailor their services accordingly.

Industry Standards and Expectations: As the industry matures, so do the expectations of clients. Pet owners now seek out dog walkers who not only love dogs but also demonstrate professionalism, reliability, and a genuine commitment to the well-being of their furry clients. This shift has elevated the standards within the industry, encouraging dog walkers to continuously improve their skills and services.

Benefits of Starting a Dog Walking Business

Passion-Driven Career: For many dog lovers, starting a dog walking business is more than just a job—it's a passion-driven career. It allows individuals to turn their love for animals into a fulfilling livelihood. The joy of spending time with dogs, witnessing their happiness during walks, and forming bonds with them and their owners can be immensely rewarding.

Flexible Schedule: One of the biggest perks of running a dog walking business is the flexibility it offers. Unlike traditional 9-to-5 jobs, dog walkers can often set their own schedules based on their availability and the needs of their clients. This flexibility is especially appealing to those seeking work-life balance or looking to supplement their income with a side business.

Low Startup Costs: Compared to many other businesses, the startup costs for a dog walking business are relatively low. Initial expenses typically include basic supplies like leashes, waste bags, and possibly insurance and marketing materials. This accessibility makes it an attractive option for aspiring entrepreneurs who may be starting on a limited budget.

Growing Demand: The demand for dog walking services continues to grow steadily, presenting ample opportunities for business expansion and sustainability. As more people recognize the importance of regular exercise and mental stimulation for their pets, they increasingly turn to professional dog walkers to meet these needs. This trend not only ensures a consistent client base but also opens doors for diversifying service offerings, such as pet sitting or specialized care.

Understanding the Demand for Dog Walking Services

Changing Lifestyles: Modern lifestyles often involve longer work hours, commuting, and other commitments that leave pet owners with less time to dedicate to their dogs' exercise needs. This shift has created a significant demand for reliable dog walking services that can bridge the gap between busy schedules and responsible pet ownership.

Health and Well-being: Regular exercise is crucial for a dog's physical health and mental well-being. Dogs, particularly those in urban environments or confined to apartments, rely on daily walks to maintain their overall fitness and prevent behavioral issues that can arise from boredom or excess energy. Pet owners understand the importance of these walks not only for their dogs' health but also for fostering a strong bond and trust between them.

Peace of Mind: For many pet owners, hiring a professional dog walker offers peace of mind knowing that their pets are in capable hands. They can rest assured that their dogs will receive the exercise, attention, and care they need, even when they are unable to be there themselves. This assurance is particularly valuable during long workdays, vacations, or times when unexpected commitments arise.

In summary, the dog walking industry combines passion, practicality, and a genuine commitment to animal welfare. By understanding the evolving needs of pet owners, embracing the joys of working with dogs, and leveraging the growing demand for professional services, aspiring dog walkers can embark on a fulfilling journey that benefits both humans and their beloved canine companions. As you continue reading, you will delve deeper into the essential steps and considerations for launching and operating a successful dog walking business.

Chapter 2: Research and Planning

Conducting Market Research

Before embarking on any business venture, conducting thorough market research is essential to understand the dynamics of the industry and identify opportunities for success. In the case of starting a dog walking business, effective market research involves gathering and analyzing data that will guide your decisions and strategies.

Understanding the Local Market: Start by assessing the demand for dog walking services in your local area. Look at demographic factors such as the number of households with dogs, average income levels, and lifestyle trends. Identify neighborhoods or communities where pet ownership is prevalent and where there might be a higher demand for dog walking services.

Competitor Analysis: Research existing dog walking businesses in your area. Identify their strengths, weaknesses, pricing strategies, and service offerings. This analysis will help you differentiate your business by offering unique services or targeting underserved niches.

Client Needs and Preferences: Conduct surveys or interviews with pet owners to understand their preferences when it comes to dog walking services. Learn about their expectations regarding reliability, frequency of walks, additional services (such as pet sitting or training), and pricing sensitivity. This insight will help you tailor your services to meet the specific needs of your target market.

Industry Trends: Stay informed about trends in the pet care industry, including advancements in technology (such as pet tracking devices or scheduling apps), changes in consumer behavior, and emerging service trends (like eco-friendly dog products or specialized training services). Adapting to these trends can give your business a competitive edge and attract more clients.

Identifying Your Target Market

Once you've gathered sufficient market data, it's time to define your target market—the specific group of pet owners who are most likely to use your dog walking services. Effective targeting allows you to focus your marketing efforts and resources on reaching the right audience.

Demographic Segmentation: Segment your target market based on demographic factors such as age, income level, occupation, and family size. For instance, busy professionals with high disposable income and dual-income families may be more willing to pay for premium dog walking services.

Psychographic Analysis: Consider the psychographic characteristics of your target market, including lifestyle preferences, values, and interests. Some pet owners may prioritize eco-friendly services, while others may seek personalized care and attention for their dogs.

Geographic Focus: Determine the geographic areas you will serve based on population density, accessibility, and competition. Consider offering services in neighborhoods with a high concentration of dog owners or areas where there is a lack of existing dog walking businesses.

Behavioral Insights: Understand the behavior and purchasing patterns of your target market. Are they frequent travelers who need reliable pet care during trips? Do they work long hours and require daily dog walking services? Tailor your service offerings and marketing messages to address these specific needs and preferences.

Analyzing Your Competition

A comprehensive analysis of your competitors provides valuable insights into their strengths and weaknesses, allowing you to differentiate your dog walking business effectively.

Identify Competitors: List all existing dog walking businesses in your area, including independent walkers, franchises, and pet care companies. Visit their websites, social media pages, and customer reviews to gather information about their services, pricing, and client feedback.

SWOT Analysis: Conduct a SWOT (Strengths, Weaknesses, Opportunities, Threats) analysis for each competitor. Identify what sets them apart from others in the market, areas where they may be lacking, and potential opportunities or threats they face. Use this analysis to position your business uniquely and capitalize on gaps in the market.

Unique Selling Proposition (USP): Determine your USP—what makes your dog walking services stand out from the competition. Whether it's specialized training, flexible scheduling, personalized care plans, or exceptional customer service, your USP should resonate with your target market and compel them to choose your services over others.

Setting Business Goals

Setting clear and achievable goals is crucial for guiding your dog walking business towards success and measuring your progress along the way.

SMART Goals: Make sure your goals are Specific, Measurable, Achievable, Relevant, and Time-bound. For example, set a goal to acquire a specific number of clients within the first six months of operation or achieve a certain revenue target by the end of the year.

Financial Objectives: Define your financial objectives, including revenue targets, profit margins, and budget allocation for marketing and operational expenses. Monitor your financial performance regularly and adjust your strategies as needed to ensure financial sustainability and growth.

Operational Milestones: Establish operational milestones such as hiring additional staff, expanding service offerings, or improving customer satisfaction metrics. These milestones provide tangible benchmarks for tracking your business's progress and celebrating achievements.

Personal Development: Consider personal development goals related to your skills, knowledge, and leadership abilities as a business owner. Investing in ongoing learning and professional development will enhance your ability to manage and grow your dog walking business effectively.

By conducting thorough research and thoughtful planning, you lay a solid foundation for your dog walking business, positioning yourself for long-term success in a competitive and rewarding industry. The insights gained from market research, understanding your target market, analyzing competitors, and setting SMART goals will guide your strategic decisions and foster growth as you launch and expand your business.

Chapter 3: Developing a Business Plan

Components of a Solid Business Plan

A well-crafted business plan serves as the roadmap for your dog walking business, outlining your vision, goals, strategies, and operational details. It not only helps you clarify your business concept but also demonstrates your readiness to potential investors or lenders. Here are the key components to include in your business plan:

Executive Summary: This section provides a concise overview of your business concept, highlighting the market opportunity, unique selling proposition (USP), target market, and financial projections. Although it appears first in the document, it is often written last, summarizing the entire business plan.

Business Description: Describe your dog walking business in detail, including the services you will offer, your target market, geographic area served, and any unique aspects of your business that set you apart from competitors.

Market Analysis: Present your findings from market research, including an assessment of the demand for dog walking services in your area, competitor analysis, and insights into consumer behavior and preferences. Demonstrate a clear understanding of your industry and target market.

Organization and Management: Outline the structure of your business, including whether you will operate as a sole proprietorship, partnership, LLC, or corporation. Introduce key team members and their roles, highlighting their relevant experience and qualifications.

Service Offering: Provide detailed information about the dog walking services you will offer, including pricing, packages, and any additional services such as pet sitting, grooming, or training. Clearly define how your services meet the needs of your target market.

Marketing and Sales Strategy: Outline your plan for attracting and retaining clients. This includes your pricing strategy, promotional activities (such as social media marketing, partnerships with local businesses, or attending pet-related events), and customer retention strategies (such as loyalty programs or referral incentives).

Financial Projections: Present detailed financial forecasts, including income statements, cash flow projections, and a break-even analysis. Estimate your startup costs and ongoing expenses, and project your revenue based on market demand and pricing strategy.

Funding Request: If you are seeking funding or financing, clearly state the amount you need, how you will use the funds, and the expected return on investment for potential investors or lenders.

Appendices: Include any additional documents that support your business plan, such as resumes of key team members, lease agreements, market research data, or legal documents.

Financial Planning and Budgeting

Effective financial planning is crucial for the success and sustainability of your dog walking business. It involves estimating your startup costs, managing cash flow, and projecting future financial performance. Here's how to approach financial planning and budgeting:

Startup Costs: Identify and list all expenses associated with launching your business, including licensing and permits, insurance premiums, equipment (such as leashes, waste bags, and GPS trackers), marketing materials, and initial working capital for operational expenses.

Operating Expenses: Estimate your ongoing monthly expenses, including rent (if applicable), utilities, payroll (if hiring employees), insurance premiums, marketing and advertising costs, and other overhead expenses. Be realistic and conservative in your estimates to ensure financial stability.

Revenue Projections: Forecast your revenue based on your pricing strategy, target market size, and anticipated demand for your services. Consider seasonal fluctuations and other factors that may impact your business's income.

Cash Flow Management: Develop a cash flow forecast to track the flow of money in and out of your business. This will help you anticipate any cash shortages and plan accordingly to ensure you have enough funds to cover expenses during lean periods.

Financial Controls: Implement financial controls to monitor and manage your business's finances effectively. This includes maintaining accurate records, reconciling bank accounts regularly, and reviewing financial reports (such as profit and loss statements) to track your business's financial performance.

Setting Short-Term and Long-Term Goals

Setting clear and achievable goals is essential for guiding your dog walking business's growth and measuring your progress over time. Here's how to set meaningful goals:

Short-Term Goals: Set goals that you aim to achieve within the first year of operation. These may include acquiring a certain number of clients, achieving a specific revenue target, establishing brand awareness in your local community, and refining your service offerings based on client feedback.

Long-Term Goals: Define your long-term objectives that extend beyond the first year. These goals may include expanding your service area, hiring additional staff, offering new pet care services (such as pet grooming or training), achieving profitability, and becoming a recognized leader in the local pet care industry.

SMART Goals: Ensure your goals are Specific, Measurable, Achievable, Relevant, and Time-bound. Break down each goal into actionable steps and set deadlines for achieving milestones along the way.

Regular Review and Adjustment: Regularly review your progress towards your goals and adjust your strategies as needed based on market conditions, client feedback, and financial performance. Celebrate achievements and learn from challenges to continuously improve your business operations.

By developing a comprehensive business plan, conducting thorough financial planning and budgeting, and setting SMART goals, you lay a solid foundation for launching and growing your dog walking business. These strategic tools will guide your decisions, attract investors or lenders, and position your business for long-term success in the competitive pet care industry.

Chapter 4: Legal Requirements and Permits

Understanding Local Regulations

Navigating the legal landscape is crucial when starting a dog walking business to ensure compliance with local regulations and avoid potential legal pitfalls. Here's what you need to know about local regulations:

Zoning Laws: Check local zoning laws to determine if you can operate a dog walking business from your home or if there are specific areas where commercial pet care services are permitted. Some neighborhoods or municipalities may have restrictions on operating businesses from residential properties.

Business Permits and Licenses: Research the specific permits and licenses required to operate a dog walking business in your area. This may include a general business license from your city or county government, as well as specialized permits for handling animals or operating a pet care facility.

Insurance Requirements: Understand the insurance requirements for dog walking businesses in your locality. Liability insurance is typically recommended to protect against claims arising from accidents or injuries that may occur while walking clients' dogs.

Health and Safety Regulations: Familiarize yourself with any health and safety regulations that apply to pet care services. This may include protocols for handling animals, maintaining cleanliness and hygiene, and ensuring the well-being of the dogs under your care.

Tax Obligations: Consult with a tax advisor or accountant to understand your tax obligations as a small business owner. This includes registering for federal, state, and local taxes, as well as understanding deductions and credits available to pet care businesses.

Registering Your Business

Registering your dog walking business establishes its legal identity and ensures compliance with government regulations. Follow these steps to register your business:

Choose a Business Name: Select a unique and memorable name for your dog walking business. Ensure the name is not already in use by another business and check if the domain name is available for a website.

Business Structure: Decide on a legal structure for your business, such as sole proprietorship, partnership, LLC (Limited Liability Company), or corporation. Each structure has different legal and tax implications, so choose the one that best suits your needs.

Register with the State: Register your business with the appropriate state agency. This may involve filing articles of incorporation or articles of organization for an LLC, depending on your chosen business structure.

Obtain an Employer Identification Number (EIN): Apply for an EIN from the IRS, even if you don't plan to hire employees immediately. An EIN is required for tax purposes and opening a business bank account.

Local Business License: Apply for a general business license from your city or county government. Provide any required documentation, pay the applicable fees, and adhere to any additional requirements, such as zoning approvals or health inspections.

Obtaining Necessary Permits and Licenses

In addition to a general business license, specific permits and licenses may be required to legally operate a dog walking business. Here's what you may need to obtain:

Animal Care Permits: Some jurisdictions require permits specifically for handling animals, including dogs. These permits may involve demonstrating knowledge of animal care, ensuring proper facilities and equipment, and adhering to health and safety regulations.

Professional Certifications: Consider obtaining certifications or training in pet first aid, dog behavior and handling, or other relevant areas. While not always required, certifications can enhance your credibility and reassure clients of your competence.

Insurance Coverage: Purchase liability insurance tailored to pet care businesses. This insurance protects you in case of accidents or injuries involving the dogs under your care, as well as damage to property or third-party injuries.

Local Health Department Approvals: Depending on your location, you may need approvals from the local health department or animal control agency. This may include inspections of your facilities and adherence to health and safety standards for pet care services.

Compliance with Industry Standards: Stay informed about industry standards and best practices for dog walking businesses. This includes guidelines for animal welfare, customer service, and business ethics to maintain a positive reputation in the community.

Navigating the legal requirements and obtaining necessary permits and licenses for your dog walking business ensures that you operate legally and responsibly. By understanding and complying with local regulations, registering your business, and obtaining the required permits and licenses, you set a solid foundation for building a successful and reputable dog walking business in your community.

Chapter 5: Choosing a Business Structure

Sole Proprietorship vs. LLC vs. Corporation

Choosing the right business structure is a critical decision when starting a dog walking business. Each structure—sole proprietorship, LLC (Limited Liability Company), and corporation—offers different benefits and considerations. Here's a detailed look at each option:

Sole Proprietorship

Definition: A sole proprietorship is the simplest form of business ownership, where you are the sole owner and operator of the business. There is no legal distinction between you and your business entity.

Pros:

- **Ease of Formation:** Setting up a sole proprietorship is straightforward and requires minimal paperwork. You can start operating your dog walking business quickly and with low startup costs.
- **Full Control:** You have complete control over business decisions and operations, allowing you to make quick decisions without needing approval from other shareholders or partners.
- **Tax Simplicity:** Income from the business is typically reported on your personal tax return (Schedule C), simplifying tax filing and compliance.

Cons:

- **Unlimited Liability:** As a sole proprietor, you are personally liable for any debts, obligations, or legal liabilities of the

business. Your personal assets (such as savings or property) are at risk in case of lawsuits or business debts.
- **Limited Growth Potential:** Sole proprietorships may face challenges in raising capital or attracting investors, limiting opportunities for business expansion.
- **Perceived Credibility:** Some clients or business partners may perceive a sole proprietorship as less credible or stable compared to other business structures.

LLC (Limited Liability Company)

Definition: An LLC combines the simplicity of a sole proprietorship with the limited liability protection of a corporation. It is a popular choice for small businesses, including dog walking businesses.

Pros:

- **Limited Liability:** The primary advantage of an LLC is that it provides personal liability protection. This means your personal assets are generally protected from business debts or legal liabilities incurred by the LLC.
- **Flexible Taxation:** LLCs have flexibility in how they are taxed. By default, they are taxed as pass-through entities where profits and losses are reported on the owners' personal tax returns. Alternatively, an LLC can elect to be taxed as a corporation.
- **Credibility:** Operating as an LLC may enhance your business's credibility and professionalism in the eyes of clients, partners, and investors.

Cons:

- **Complexity and Cost:** Forming and maintaining an LLC typically involves more paperwork and costs compared to a sole proprietorship. You may need to file articles of organization,

create an operating agreement, and comply with ongoing state requirements.
- **Limited Growth Potential:** While an LLC offers more flexibility than a sole proprietorship, it may still face challenges in raising capital or attracting investors compared to a corporation.

Corporation

Definition: A corporation is a separate legal entity from its owners (shareholders), providing the highest level of personal liability protection and potential for growth and investment.

Pros:

- **Limited Liability:** Shareholders are generally not personally liable for the debts or legal obligations of the corporation. Personal assets are protected, which is a significant advantage in case of lawsuits or business debts.
- **Access to Capital:** Corporations can raise capital by issuing shares of stock to investors. This makes it easier to attract investment and finance business growth.
- **Perpetual Existence:** A corporation has perpetual existence, meaning its existence is not affected by changes in ownership or the death of shareholders.

Cons:

- **Complexity:** Corporations are more complex and costly to establish and maintain than sole proprietorships or LLCs. You must comply with state incorporation requirements, hold regular shareholder meetings, and maintain detailed corporate records.
- **Double Taxation:** C corporations may face double taxation, where the corporation pays taxes on its profits, and

shareholders pay taxes on dividends received. However, this can be mitigated by careful tax planning and structuring.

Choosing the Right Structure for Your Business

When deciding on the best structure for your dog walking business, consider the following factors:

Liability Protection: Evaluate your personal risk tolerance and the level of protection you need for your personal assets. If minimizing personal liability is a priority, an LLC or corporation may be more suitable than a sole proprietorship.

Tax Implications: Consider the tax advantages and implications of each business structure. Consult with a tax advisor to understand how each structure will impact your tax obligations, deductions, and potential for tax savings.

Business Goals: Align your choice of business structure with your long-term goals for growth, expansion, and succession planning. If you anticipate significant growth or plan to attract investors, a corporation may provide the best framework.

Operational Needs: Assess the administrative requirements, ongoing compliance obligations, and costs associated with each business structure. Choose a structure that allows you to operate efficiently while meeting legal and regulatory requirements.

Legal Advice: Seek guidance from a qualified attorney or business advisor who can provide personalized advice based on your specific circumstances, local regulations, and industry norms.

Choosing the right business structure is a foundational step in establishing your dog walking business. By understanding the pros and cons of sole proprietorship, LLC, and corporation, and aligning your choice with your business goals and operational needs, you can lay a solid foundation for long-term success and growth in the competitive pet care industry.

Chapter 6: Setting Up Your Business

Finding a Suitable Location (if Applicable)

Deciding where to operate your dog walking business is an important consideration that can impact your accessibility to clients, operational efficiency, and overall success. Whether you choose to operate from a physical location or run your business from home, here are key factors to consider:

Physical Location: If you decide to establish a physical location for your dog walking business, consider the following:

- **Accessibility:** Choose a location that is easily accessible to your target market of pet owners. This may be in a residential neighborhood with a high concentration of dog owners or near popular dog-friendly parks and walking trails.
- **Visibility:** A visible location can attract walk-in clients and enhance your business's visibility within the community. Consider locations with high foot traffic or where pet-related businesses (such as veterinary clinics or pet supply stores) are clustered.
- **Space Requirements:** Assess your space needs based on the size of your operation. You may need a storefront with space for client consultations, a waiting area, and storage for equipment such as leashes, waste bags, and cleaning supplies.
- **Zoning and Permits:** Ensure the location is zoned appropriately for pet care services and obtain any necessary permits or licenses from local authorities.

Compliance with zoning regulations is crucial to avoid potential legal issues.

Home Office Setup: Running a dog walking business from home offers flexibility and cost savings. Here's how to set up a productive home office:

- **Designated Workspace:** Dedicate a specific area of your home for business activities. Ideally, choose a quiet and distraction-free space where you can focus on administrative tasks, client communications, and scheduling.
- **Equipment and Supplies:** Equip your home office with essential tools and supplies, including a computer, printer, phone line dedicated to business calls, filing cabinets or storage bins for paperwork, and a comfortable workspace.
- **Internet and Communication:** Ensure reliable internet access for managing online bookings, email communications with clients, and maintaining a professional online presence. Consider setting up a separate business email address and phone number for client inquiries.
- **Legal Considerations:** Check local regulations regarding home-based businesses, including zoning restrictions and any permits required. Inform your homeowners' association (if applicable) about your business activities to ensure compliance with neighborhood rules.

Organizing Your Workspace

An organized workspace is essential for efficiency, productivity, and creating a positive impression on clients. Follow these tips to organize your workspace effectively:

Storage Solutions: Use storage bins, shelves, or cabinets to keep your workspace clutter-free and organized. Store equipment and supplies such as leashes, waste bags, and grooming tools in labeled containers for easy access.

Desk Organization: Keep your desk tidy and organized. Use desk organizers, trays, or filing systems to manage paperwork, client contracts, scheduling calendars, and financial records. Establish a filing system that categorizes documents by client, financial year, or business expenses.

Client Area: If you meet clients at your home office or physical location, create a welcoming and professional client area. Provide comfortable seating, water bowls for visiting dogs, and informational materials about your services.

Sanitation and Cleanliness: Maintain a clean and hygienic workspace, especially if handling pets or meeting clients at your location. Regularly disinfect surfaces, wash pet-related equipment, and ensure proper waste disposal for used waste bags.

Decor and Ambiance: Personalize your workspace with decor that reflects your brand and creates a welcoming atmosphere for clients and pets. Consider pet-friendly decorations, calming colors, and ambient lighting to create a positive environment.

Technology Integration: Integrate technology solutions to streamline business operations. Use scheduling software for managing appointments, invoicing tools for billing clients, and customer relationship management (CRM) systems to track client preferences and feedback.

Conclusion

Setting up your dog walking business involves thoughtful planning and organization to create a functional and inviting workspace. Whether you choose a physical location or operate from home, prioritize accessibility, organization, and professionalism to enhance client satisfaction and operational efficiency. By finding a suitable location (if applicable), setting up a home office, and organizing your workspace effectively, you establish a solid foundation for delivering exceptional pet care services and growing your business in the competitive pet industry landscape.

Chapter 7: Insurance and Liability

Importance of Insurance for a Dog Walking Business

Insurance is a vital aspect of protecting your dog walking business from potential risks and liabilities. As a pet care provider, you are responsible for the safety and well-being of the dogs in your care, as well as the satisfaction of your clients. Here's why insurance is crucial:

Risk Management: Operating a dog walking business involves inherent risks, such as accidents, injuries to dogs or third parties, property damage, or legal disputes. Insurance provides financial protection against these risks, minimizing the impact on your business and personal finances.

Client Confidence: Having appropriate insurance coverage demonstrates professionalism and accountability to your clients. It reassures them that you are prepared to handle unexpected situations and fulfill your obligations in case of accidents or unforeseen events.

Legal Requirements: Depending on your location and the services you offer, certain types of insurance may be required by law or industry regulations. Compliance with insurance requirements ensures you operate legally and avoid potential penalties or legal liabilities.

Business Continuity: Insurance coverage can help your dog walking business recover quickly from incidents that could otherwise disrupt operations or lead to financial strain. This includes covering costs for medical expenses, legal fees, and damages resulting from covered incidents.

Types of Insurance Coverage Needed

When choosing insurance coverage for your dog walking business, consider the following types of policies that provide comprehensive protection:

General Liability Insurance:

- **Coverage:** Protects against claims of bodily injury or property damage to third parties (clients, bystanders, or property owners) caused by your business activities. This includes incidents that occur during dog walks or interactions with clients in public spaces.
- **Importance:** General liability insurance is essential for addressing common risks in pet care services, such as a dog causing injury to a passerby or damaging someone's property.

Professional Liability Insurance (Errors and Omissions Insurance):

- **Coverage:** Covers claims of negligence, errors, or omissions in the professional services you provide. This may include allegations of inadequate care, failure to follow client instructions, or misinformation provided to clients.
- **Importance:** Professional liability insurance protects your business from financial losses associated with legal defense costs and settlements resulting from claims of professional negligence.

Commercial Property Insurance:

- **Coverage:** Protects your business property, including equipment, supplies, and furniture, against damage or loss due to covered perils such as fire, theft, vandalism, or natural disasters.

- **Importance:** If you operate from a physical location (office or storefront), commercial property insurance safeguards your assets and ensures continuity of business operations in case of unexpected events.

Animal Bailee Coverage:

- **Coverage:** Covers veterinary expenses or medical bills for dogs in your care if they are injured, become ill, or die due to covered incidents. It may also cover expenses related to lost or stolen pets.
- **Importance:** Animal bailee coverage is crucial for dog walking businesses to protect against liability for injuries or health emergencies that occur while pets are under your supervision.

Workers' Compensation Insurance:

- **Coverage:** Provides wage replacement and medical benefits to employees who are injured or become ill while performing work-related duties. It also protects your business from potential lawsuits related to workplace injuries.
- **Importance:** If you hire employees or independent contractors to assist with dog walking or pet care services, workers' compensation insurance is typically required by law in most states to protect both employees and your business.

Finding the Right Insurance Provider

Choosing the right insurance provider is essential for obtaining reliable coverage and support for your dog walking business. Consider these factors when selecting an insurance provider:

Industry Expertise: Look for insurance providers with experience in the pet care industry. They should understand the unique risks and challenges faced by dog walking businesses and offer tailored insurance solutions.

Coverage Options: Evaluate the types of insurance policies offered by each provider and ensure they meet the specific needs of your business. Seek comprehensive coverage that addresses potential risks associated with dog walking and pet care services.

Financial Stability: Choose an insurance company with a strong financial rating and a history of prompt claims processing and customer service. Verify their reputation and reliability through client testimonials and industry reviews.

Cost and Affordability: Compare premium rates, deductibles, and coverage limits from multiple insurance providers to find a policy that offers the best value for your budget. Avoid choosing solely based on price; prioritize comprehensive coverage and reliable service.

Customer Support: Assess the quality of customer service and support provided by each insurance provider. A responsive and knowledgeable insurance agent can help you understand policy terms, coverage options, and claims procedures.

Claims Process: Understand the claims filing process and how quickly claims are processed and resolved. Choose an insurance provider known for fair claims handling and timely reimbursement for covered losses.

Legal Compliance: Ensure the insurance provider is licensed to sell insurance in your state and complies with all regulatory requirements. Verify their credentials and confirm they have a good standing with state insurance departments.

Conclusion

Securing appropriate insurance coverage is a critical step in safeguarding your dog walking business against potential risks and liabilities. By understanding the importance of insurance, identifying the types of coverage needed (such as general liability, professional liability, commercial property, animal bailee, and workers' compensation insurance), and choosing a reputable insurance provider, you protect your business's financial stability and reputation. Prioritize comprehensive coverage that aligns with your business needs and risk tolerance, ensuring peace of mind as you provide exceptional pet care services to clients in your community.

Chapter 8: Creating a Brand Identity

Choosing a Business Name

Selecting a business name is more than just a label; it's the foundation of your brand identity. Your business name should reflect your services, resonate with potential clients, and set the tone for your brand's personality. Here's how to choose a memorable and effective business name for your dog walking business:

Reflect Your Services: Incorporate keywords that clearly indicate what your business offers. Consider terms like "paws," "walks," "pets," or "rover" to highlight your focus on dog walking services.

Unique and Memorable: Choose a name that stands out from competitors and is easy to remember. Avoid overly complex or obscure names that may confuse potential clients.

Check Availability: Ensure the business name is available as a domain name for your website and across social media platforms. Verify trademark availability to avoid legal issues and potential conflicts with existing businesses.

Consider Brand Expansion: Think long-term about how your business name will resonate if you expand services beyond dog walking, such as pet sitting or grooming.

Feedback and Testing: Gather feedback from friends, family, and potential clients to gauge their impressions of the business name. Test different options to see which resonates best with your target audience.

Designing a Logo

A well-designed logo serves as the visual representation of your brand and helps establish a professional and cohesive identity. Here's how to create a compelling logo for your dog walking business:

Simple and Recognizable: Opt for a clean and simple design that is easy to recognize and scalable for different applications (e.g., business cards, website, apparel).

Incorporate Pet Themes: Use elements like paw prints, dog silhouettes, or playful fonts that convey your connection to pets and pet care.

Color Psychology: Choose colors that evoke emotions and align with your brand's personality. For example, blue can convey trust and reliability, while green may represent freshness and outdoor activities.

Professional Design Tools: Consider hiring a graphic designer or using online design tools to create a professional-looking logo. Ensure the logo is versatile and works well in both color and black-and-white formats.

Feedback and Iteration: Seek feedback from clients and peers to refine your logo design. Make adjustments based on constructive criticism to ensure your logo effectively communicates your brand's identity.

Creating a Brand Message and Mission Statement

Crafting a compelling brand message and mission statement communicates your business's values, goals, and commitment to clients. It sets the tone for how you interact with clients and the community. Here's how to develop a meaningful brand message and mission statement:

Define Your Values: Identify the core values that drive your dog walking business, such as trust, reliability, compassion for animals, and exceptional customer service.

Unique Selling Proposition (USP): Highlight what sets your dog walking services apart from competitors. Emphasize unique benefits, such as personalized care plans, GPS tracking for walks, or additional pet care services.

Client-Centric Approach: Focus on the needs and preferences of your target clients. Your brand message should resonate with pet owners who value reliability, safety, and genuine care for their dogs.

Mission Statement: Summarize your business's purpose and objectives in a concise mission statement. Clearly articulate how you aim to improve the lives of pets and pet owners through your services.

Authenticity and Consistency: Ensure your brand message and mission statement authentically reflect your values and are consistently communicated across all marketing channels, including your website, social media, and client communications.

Inspire Trust: Use language that inspires confidence and trust in your services. Demonstrate your commitment to excellence and professionalism in every aspect of your business operations.

Conclusion

Creating a strong brand identity is essential for establishing credibility, attracting clients, and building a loyal customer base for your dog walking business. By carefully selecting a business name that reflects your services, designing a memorable logo, and crafting a compelling brand message and mission statement, you set the stage for differentiation and recognition in the competitive pet care industry. Invest time in developing a cohesive brand identity that resonates with pet owners and communicates your dedication to providing exceptional dog walking services. Your brand identity will not only differentiate you from competitors but also create a lasting impression that encourages client trust and loyalty.

Chapter 9: Pricing Your Services

Determining Your Pricing Strategy

Setting the right prices for your dog walking services requires careful consideration of various factors, including your business expenses, market demand, competitor rates, and perceived value by clients. Here's how to develop an effective pricing strategy:

Cost Analysis: Start by calculating your business expenses, including insurance premiums, marketing costs, transportation expenses, and any equipment or supplies needed for dog walking. Determine your desired profit margin to cover these costs and generate a reasonable income.

Market Research: Research prevailing rates for dog walking services in your local area. Consider factors such as service duration (e.g., 30-minute vs. 60-minute walks), additional services (e.g., solo walks, group walks, or special care for senior dogs), and geographic location (urban vs. suburban areas).

Competitive Analysis: Analyze pricing strategies used by competitors offering similar dog walking services. Identify businesses that target the same clientele and compare their pricing structures, service offerings, and unique value propositions.

Value-Based Pricing: Determine the unique value your services offer to clients. Highlight factors like personalized attention, certified pet care professionals, GPS tracking of walks, or additional perks that justify higher pricing compared to competitors.

Profitability Goals: Set clear financial goals for your business, such as monthly revenue targets and profit margins. Ensure your pricing strategy aligns with these goals while remaining competitive within the local market.

Researching Market Rates

Gathering accurate information about market rates for dog walking services is essential for making informed pricing decisions. Here are effective ways to conduct market research:

Online Platforms: Explore online directories, pet care service websites, and social media platforms to gather information on rates charged by local dog walking businesses. Review client reviews and testimonials to understand perceived value and service quality.

Local Networking: Attend pet-related events, networking meetings, or community gatherings where pet owners and pet care professionals gather. Engage in conversations to learn about typical rates and client expectations for dog walking services in your area.

Survey Potential Clients: Conduct surveys or informal interviews with pet owners in your target demographic. Ask questions about their preferences for dog walking services, willingness to pay for premium services, and factors influencing their decision-making process.

Professional Associations: Join pet care associations or organizations that provide industry insights and resources. Participate in forums or webinars to gain knowledge about pricing trends, best practices, and regulatory considerations for dog walking businesses.

Consult Industry Experts: Seek advice from experienced pet care professionals, business advisors, or mentors who can offer guidance based on their knowledge of the local market and industry benchmarks.

Creating Pricing Packages

Developing structured pricing packages can simplify client decision-making and enhance the perceived value of your services. Here's how to create appealing pricing packages for your dog walking business:

Tiered Pricing: Offer different service tiers based on duration (e.g., 30-minute, 60-minute walks), frequency (e.g., daily, weekly packages), or additional services (e.g., solo walks, pet taxi service, basic grooming).

Bundle Services: Bundle related services together to create value-packed packages. For example, offer discounted rates for clients who purchase monthly packages or recurring service contracts.

Specialized Services: Introduce specialized services tailored to specific client needs or preferences. Examples include puppy socialization walks, senior dog care, training reinforcement sessions, or adventure hikes in nearby parks.

Promotional Offers: Launch promotional offers or seasonal discounts to attract new clients and encourage repeat business. Consider offering referral incentives or loyalty rewards for clients who book recurring services or refer friends and family.

Transparent Pricing: Clearly outline the details of each pricing package, including service inclusions, pricing structure (hourly rates or flat fees), cancellation policies, and payment terms. Transparency builds trust and reduces confusion for potential clients.

Upsell Opportunities: Identify opportunities to upsell premium services or add-ons, such as pet sitting, overnight stays, or personalized training sessions. Highlight the benefits of these additional services to justify higher pricing tiers.

Conclusion

Pricing your dog walking services effectively requires a strategic approach that balances profitability with competitive positioning and client expectations. By conducting thorough market research, understanding local market rates, and developing structured pricing packages that highlight your unique value proposition, you can attract clients, maximize revenue, and build a sustainable business in the pet care industry. Continuously evaluate and adjust your pricing strategy based on market dynamics, client feedback, and business growth goals to maintain competitiveness and profitability over time. Your pricing strategy should reflect your commitment to delivering exceptional dog walking services while meeting the diverse needs of pet owners in your community.

Chapter 10: Marketing Your Dog Walking Business

Developing a Marketing Plan

A well-crafted marketing plan is essential for promoting your dog walking business, attracting clients, and establishing a strong market presence. Here's how to develop an effective marketing strategy:

Identify Your Target Audience: Define your ideal clients based on demographics (age, location, lifestyle), psychographics (pet ownership behavior, preferences), and specific needs for dog walking services.

Unique Selling Proposition (USP): Highlight what sets your dog walking services apart from competitors. Emphasize factors like personalized care, certified pet care professionals, flexible scheduling options, or additional perks (e.g., GPS tracking of walks).

Set Marketing Goals: Establish clear, measurable objectives for your marketing efforts, such as increasing client inquiries, booking rates, or website traffic. Define timelines and benchmarks to track progress and evaluate the effectiveness of your strategies.

Choose Marketing Channels: Select marketing channels that align with your target audience and budget. Consider a mix of online (social media, website, online directories) and offline (local community events, flyers, partnerships with pet-related businesses) strategies.

Budget Allocation: Allocate resources for marketing activities, including advertising expenses, website development, graphic design for promotional materials, and professional photography for branding purposes.

Marketing Messages: Craft compelling marketing messages that resonate with pet owners' needs and preferences. Emphasize trustworthiness, reliability, and genuine care for their pets to establish emotional connections and build client trust.

Monitor and Evaluate: Continuously monitor the performance of your marketing campaigns using analytics tools (e.g., Google Analytics, social media insights). Analyze key metrics such as website traffic, engagement rates, conversion rates, and return on investment (ROI).

Utilizing Social Media

Social media platforms offer powerful tools for connecting with pet owners, showcasing your expertise, and promoting your dog walking services. Here's how to leverage social media effectively:

Choose Relevant Platforms: Identify the social media platforms most frequented by your target audience, such as Facebook, Instagram, Twitter, or TikTok. Tailor your content strategy to each platform's unique features and audience demographics.

Content Strategy: Create engaging content that educates, entertains, and inspires pet owners. Share tips on dog care, highlight client testimonials, showcase happy dogs on walks, and behind-the-scenes glimpses of your daily activities.

Visual Appeal: Use high-quality photos and videos to capture attention and showcase your dog walking services. Include captions that reinforce your brand's personality, values, and commitment to pet care excellence.

Engagement and Interaction: Foster community engagement by responding to comments, messages, and inquiries promptly. Encourage clients to share their experiences and testimonials on social media, amplifying word-of-mouth referrals.

Hashtags and Geotags: Use relevant hashtags (#dogwalking, #petcare) and geotags (location-based tags) to increase visibility and attract local pet owners searching for dog walking services in your area.

Paid Advertising: Consider using paid social media advertising to reach a broader audience and target specific demographics or geographic locations. Experiment with promoted posts, carousel ads, or video ads to showcase your services effectively.

Creating a Professional Website

A professional website serves as your online storefront and a valuable resource for potential clients to learn about your dog walking services. Here's how to create an effective website:

Clear Navigation: Design a user-friendly layout with easy navigation. Include a homepage, services page, about us section, client testimonials, contact information, and a blog or resource section for pet care tips.

Service Descriptions: Clearly outline your dog walking services, including service packages, pricing, service areas, and any additional services offered (e.g., pet sitting, grooming referrals).

Client Testimonials: Showcase positive reviews and testimonials from satisfied clients to build credibility and trust. Include photos or videos of happy dogs on walks to visually reinforce the quality of your services.

Contact Information: Display your contact information prominently on every page of your website. Include a contact form for inquiries, phone number, email address, and links to your social media profiles for easy communication.

SEO Optimization: Optimize your website for search engines (SEO) to improve visibility in local search results. Use relevant keywords (e.g., dog walking services in [your city]) throughout your website content, meta descriptions, and image alt texts.

Mobile Compatibility: Ensure your website is mobile-friendly and responsive, providing a seamless browsing experience on smartphones and tablets. Test your website's functionality across different devices and screen sizes.

Call-to-Action (CTA): Include clear CTAs prompting visitors to take action, such as scheduling a consultation, booking a dog walk, subscribing to your newsletter, or following your social media pages.

Conclusion

Effectively marketing your dog walking business involves strategic planning, leveraging social media platforms, and creating a professional online presence through your website. By developing a comprehensive marketing plan that identifies your target audience, emphasizes your unique selling proposition, and utilizes social media channels to engage with pet owners, you can attract new clients and build lasting relationships in the pet care industry. Continuously monitor your marketing efforts, adapt strategies based on performance data, and prioritize client engagement to maximize visibility and grow your dog walking business successfully. Your marketing efforts should reflect your passion for pet care and commitment to delivering exceptional services that meet the needs of pet owners seeking reliable and trustworthy dog walking providers.

Chapter 11: Networking and Building Relationships

Joining Local Business Groups and Associations

Networking within local business groups and associations is crucial for establishing connections, gaining referrals, and enhancing your reputation in the community. Here's how to effectively network as a dog walking business owner:

Research Local Groups: Identify business organizations, chambers of commerce, and industry-specific associations in your area. Choose groups that cater to pet care professionals, small businesses, or local entrepreneurs.

Attend Networking Events: Participate in networking events, seminars, workshops, and social gatherings hosted by local business groups. These events provide opportunities to meet potential clients, collaborate with fellow business owners, and exchange industry insights.

Introduce Your Services: Prepare a concise elevator pitch that highlights your dog walking services, unique selling points, and commitment to pet care excellence. Be prepared to discuss how your services can benefit pet owners and meet their specific needs.

Build Relationships: Focus on building genuine relationships with other business owners, community leaders, and potential clients. Listen actively, ask questions, and offer support or advice whenever possible to establish trust and rapport.

Exchange Business Cards: Exchange business cards with contacts you meet at networking events. Follow up with personalized emails or LinkedIn connections to continue building relationships and exploring potential collaborations.

Volunteer or Sponsor: Volunteer your time or services at local pet-related events, charity fundraisers, or community initiatives. Sponsorship opportunities can increase your visibility and demonstrate your commitment to supporting local causes.

Partnering with Pet Stores and Veterinarians

Collaborating with pet stores and veterinarians can enhance your credibility, expand your client base, and create valuable referral partnerships. Here's how to establish partnerships effectively:

Identify Potential Partners: Research pet stores, veterinary clinics, groomers, and pet supply retailers in your area. Choose businesses that share your commitment to pet care and have a positive reputation among pet owners.

Initiate Contact: Introduce yourself to store managers or veterinarians through phone calls, emails, or in-person visits. Explain your dog walking services, highlight mutual benefits of collaboration, and propose ways to work together.

Offer Value: Provide value to your partners by offering discounted services for their employees or clients, hosting informational sessions on pet care topics, or cross-promoting each other's services through joint marketing efforts.

Referral Program: Establish a formal referral program where pet stores and veterinarians refer clients in need of dog walking services to your business. Offer incentives such as discounted rates, gift cards, or mutual referrals to incentivize referrals.

Maintain Communication: Regularly communicate with your partners to nurture the relationship. Provide updates on your services, share client success stories, and express appreciation for their support in referring clients to your business.

Collaborate on Events: Organize joint events or workshops with pet stores or veterinarians, such as pet health seminars, adoption events, or pet care demonstrations. These collaborations can attract new clients and strengthen community ties.

Building a Client Referral Program

A client referral program encourages satisfied clients to recommend your dog walking services to friends, family, and colleagues, helping to generate new business through word-of-mouth referrals. Here's how to create an effective referral program:

Incentivize Referrals: Offer incentives such as discounts on future services, free walks, or gift cards for clients who refer new customers to your business. Clearly outline the referral rewards and eligibility criteria.

Promote the Program: Inform existing clients about your referral program through email newsletters, social media posts, and personalized client communications. Highlight the benefits of referring friends and emphasize your appreciation for their support.

Provide Referral Materials: Create referral cards or digital referral links that clients can easily share with their contacts. Include your contact information, website URL, and a compelling call-to-action encouraging recipients to book dog walking services.

Track Referrals: Implement a system to track referrals and monitor the effectiveness of your referral program. Use customer relationship management (CRM) software or spreadsheet tools to record referrals, track rewards, and follow up with referrers.

Acknowledge Referrers: Recognize and thank clients who refer new business to your dog walking services. Send personalized thank-you notes, offer exclusive rewards for top referrers, and publicly acknowledge their support on social media or your website.

Continuous Promotion: Continuously promote your referral program to maintain client engagement and encourage ongoing referrals. Periodically remind clients about the program's benefits and encourage them to share their positive experiences with others.

Conclusion

Networking, partnering with local businesses, and implementing a client referral program are invaluable strategies for growing your dog walking business and establishing a strong presence in the community. By actively participating in local business groups, forming partnerships with pet stores and veterinarians, and incentivizing client referrals, you can expand your client base, increase brand visibility, and build long-term relationships with pet owners. These initiatives not only enhance your credibility and reputation but also position your dog walking business for sustained growth and success in the competitive pet care industry. Continuously nurture relationships, provide exceptional service, and leverage word-of-mouth referrals to create a thriving business that meets the needs of pet owners and their beloved dogs.

Chapter 12: Creating Contracts and Agreements

Importance of Written Agreements

Establishing clear expectations and responsibilities is essential for ensuring a successful and professional relationship between your dog walking business and clients. A written contract not only protects both parties but also provides clarity on services, terms of engagement, and recourse in case of disputes. Here's why written agreements are crucial:

Clarity and Understanding: A written contract clarifies the scope of services provided, scheduling details, pricing, cancellation policies, and other essential terms. It ensures both parties have a clear understanding of their obligations and rights.

Legal Protection: Contracts serve as legal documents that outline the rights and responsibilities of each party. In case of disagreements or misunderstandings, a well-drafted contract can provide legal recourse and protect your business interests.

Professionalism: Utilizing written agreements demonstrates professionalism and commitment to delivering high-quality services. It reassures clients that you take their needs seriously and are dedicated to providing reliable and trustworthy dog walking services.

Risk Management: Clearly defined terms in a contract help mitigate risks associated with liability, disputes over payment, scheduling conflicts, or unexpected circumstances (e.g., emergencies, changes in service requirements).

Client Satisfaction: By outlining expectations upfront, contracts help manage client expectations and minimize misunderstandings. Clients feel more confident and comfortable knowing the terms of engagement are clearly documented.

Key Components of a Dog Walking Contract

When drafting a dog walking contract, include comprehensive details that address important aspects of your services and client interactions. Here are key components to include in your contract:

Service Description: Clearly describe the dog walking services you will provide, including frequency, duration of walks, any additional services (e.g., feeding, basic grooming), and special instructions for handling the client's pet.

Pricing and Payment Terms: Outline the pricing structure for your services, payment methods accepted (e.g., cash, credit card, online payments), invoicing schedules, and any late payment fees or discounts for recurring clients.

Cancellation and Refund Policies: Specify conditions under which either party can cancel services (e.g., notice period required), refund policies for prepaid services, and any penalties for last-minute cancellations by the client.

Liability and Insurance: Clarify your liability coverage and insurance policies, including disclaimers of liability for injuries to pets or property during walks. Encourage clients to provide proof of pet health insurance if applicable.

Terms of Engagement: Include terms related to access to the client's property, confidentiality of client information, and handling of keys or access codes. Address how you will handle emergencies or unforeseen circumstances.

Dispute Resolution: Outline procedures for resolving disputes, such as mediation or arbitration. Specify jurisdiction and applicable laws governing the contract to clarify legal recourse for both parties.

Termination of Agreement: Define conditions under which either party can terminate the agreement, including notice periods and reasons for termination (e.g., breach of contract, non-payment).

Client Responsibilities: Detail client responsibilities, such as providing accurate pet care instructions, ensuring pets are vaccinated and properly restrained, and notifying you of any changes in scheduling or pet health.

Managing Client Expectations

Effective communication and transparency are key to managing client expectations and fostering positive relationships. Here's how to ensure clients have realistic expectations of your dog walking services:

Initial Consultation: Conduct a thorough initial consultation with clients to discuss their pet's needs, behavioral traits, health considerations, and preferred walking schedule. Address any concerns or special requests upfront.

Service Details: Provide clients with detailed information about your services, including service limitations, safety protocols during walks, and any additional services available upon request (e.g., pet sitting, basic training reinforcement).

Communication Channels: Establish clear communication channels (e.g., phone, email, text messaging) for clients to reach you with questions, updates, or emergencies related to their pets. Respond promptly to client inquiries to build trust and reliability.

Feedback Mechanisms: Encourage clients to provide feedback on your services and communicate openly about any issues or concerns. Use client feedback to improve service delivery and demonstrate your commitment to client satisfaction.

Educational Resources: Offer educational resources or tips on dog care, behavior training, and safety measures through your website, social media channels, or client newsletters. Empower clients to make informed decisions about their pet's well-being.

Consistent Service Delivery: Strive for consistency in service delivery, adhering to agreed-upon schedules and providing updates or photos of pets during walks. Consistency builds trust and reinforces your commitment to pet care excellence.

Conclusion

Creating thorough contracts and agreements is fundamental to operating a professional and successful dog walking business. By documenting service details, outlining terms of engagement, and managing client expectations effectively, you establish a foundation of trust, clarity, and professionalism with your clients. Written agreements not only protect your business interests and mitigate risks but also ensure clients understand and agree to the terms of service. Continuously communicate with clients, solicit feedback, and uphold high standards of service delivery to foster long-term client relationships and differentiate your dog walking business in the competitive pet care industry. Your commitment to transparency, reliability, and exceptional pet care will contribute to the growth and sustainability of your business over time.

Chapter 13: Managing Finances

Setting Up a Business Bank Account

Establishing a separate business bank account is essential for managing your dog walking business's finances effectively. Here's how to set up and utilize a business bank account:

Separate Personal and Business Finances: Opening a dedicated business bank account separates your personal finances from your business transactions. This simplifies financial record-keeping, tax preparation, and monitoring of business expenses and income.

Choose the Right Bank: Research local banks or credit unions that offer business banking services tailored to small businesses. Compare account features, fees, minimum balance requirements, online banking capabilities, and accessibility to determine the best fit for your needs.

Gather Required Documentation: Prepare necessary documentation, such as your business registration or incorporation documents, employer identification number (EIN) from the IRS (if applicable), and personal identification (e.g., driver's license, passport).

Visit the Bank: Schedule an appointment or visit the bank branch to open your business bank account. Provide the required documentation, complete account opening forms, and deposit initial funds to activate your account.

Set Up Online Banking: Once your account is open, enroll in online banking services offered by the bank. Online banking allows you to monitor account activity, transfer funds, pay bills electronically, and download statements for record-keeping purposes.

Use Business Checks and Debit Cards: Order business checks and request a business debit card linked to your account. Use these payment methods for business expenses to track transactions accurately and separate personal purchases from business expenditures.

Tracking Income and Expenses

Accurate tracking of income and expenses is crucial for maintaining financial stability and making informed business decisions. Here's how to effectively manage your dog walking business finances:

Maintain Detailed Records: Keep organized records of all business income and expenses using accounting software, spreadsheets, or manual ledgers. Record each transaction promptly, including client payments, business expenses (e.g., pet supplies, advertising costs), and mileage for tax purposes.

Categorize Transactions: Create categories for income and expenses relevant to your dog walking business, such as service revenue, client payments, equipment purchases, vehicle expenses (e.g., fuel, maintenance), insurance premiums, and professional fees.

Invoice Clients Promptly: Issue invoices to clients promptly for dog walking services rendered. Include payment terms, accepted payment methods, and a due date to ensure timely payment and maintain steady cash flow.

Monitor Cash Flow: Regularly review your business bank account statements and cash flow projections to track incoming revenue and outgoing expenses. Identify any discrepancies or irregularities that require further investigation or correction.

Reconcile Accounts: Reconcile your business bank account and credit card statements monthly to verify that recorded transactions match actual bank records. Reconciliation helps identify errors, detect unauthorized transactions, and ensure accurate financial reporting.

Track Tax Obligations: Set aside funds for estimated quarterly tax payments (if applicable) based on your business income and tax bracket. Consult with a tax professional to understand tax obligations, deductions, and potential tax-saving strategies specific to your business.

Understanding Taxes and Deductions

Navigating tax responsibilities as a small business owner requires understanding applicable taxes, deductions, and compliance requirements. Here's an overview of key considerations for managing taxes:

Income Tax: Report business income on your personal tax return using Schedule C (Profit or Loss from Business). Pay income tax on net profit (income minus deductible expenses) at your individual tax rate.

Self-Employment Tax: Pay self-employment tax to cover Social Security and Medicare contributions as a self-employed individual. Calculate self-employment tax using Schedule SE (Self-Employment Tax) and include it with your tax return.

Deductible Business Expenses: Deduct eligible business expenses from your taxable income to reduce your tax liability. Common deductible expenses for dog walking businesses may include vehicle expenses (mileage, fuel, maintenance), insurance premiums, pet care supplies, marketing costs, professional fees, and home office expenses (if applicable).

Depreciation Deductions: Depreciate the cost of business assets, such as vehicles or equipment used for dog walking services, over their useful life. Use IRS guidelines and depreciation schedules to calculate allowable depreciation deductions each year.

Quarterly Estimated Taxes: If your annual tax liability is expected to exceed a certain threshold, you may need to make quarterly estimated tax payments to the IRS. Estimate taxes owed based on current year income and deductions, and submit payments by quarterly deadlines (April 15, June 15, September 15, and January 15 of the following year).

Tax Compliance: Stay informed about tax filing deadlines, reporting requirements, and changes to tax laws that may impact your dog walking business. Maintain accurate financial records, retain receipts and invoices as proof of expenses, and consult with a tax advisor or accountant for guidance on tax planning and compliance.

Conclusion

Effective financial management is essential for the long-term success and sustainability of your dog walking business. By setting up a dedicated business bank account, diligently tracking income and expenses, and understanding tax obligations and deductions, you can maintain financial stability, comply with regulatory requirements, and make informed business decisions. Consistently monitor your business finances, seek professional advice when needed, and implement best practices for record-keeping and tax planning to optimize financial performance and minimize risks. Your commitment to sound financial management practices will contribute to the growth and profitability of your dog walking business over time, ensuring you remain financially resilient in a competitive market environment.

Chapter 14: Scheduling and Time Management

Creating an Efficient Schedule

Effective scheduling and time management are crucial for maximizing productivity, meeting client needs, and maintaining work-life balance in your dog walking business. Here's how to create and manage an efficient schedule:

Understand Client Needs: Start by understanding the specific needs and preferences of each client, including preferred walking times, frequency of walks, and any special instructions for their pets. Gather this information during initial consultations and maintain detailed client profiles.

Block Scheduling: Organize your daily and weekly schedule into blocks of time dedicated to client visits, administrative tasks, and personal activities. Allocate sufficient time for each client appointment, travel between locations, and breaks to avoid scheduling conflicts.

Prioritize Tasks: Prioritize tasks based on urgency and importance. Schedule essential activities, such as client appointments, first, followed by administrative tasks (e.g., invoicing, client communications), and non-urgent activities during less busy periods.

Use a Calendar or Planner: Utilize a physical planner or digital calendar to visualize your schedule and track appointments, deadlines, and personal commitments. Choose a scheduling tool that suits your preferences and allows for easy updating and synchronization across devices.

Buffer Time: Incorporate buffer time between appointments to accommodate unforeseen delays, traffic conditions, or additional time needed for pet care tasks. Buffer time helps maintain punctuality and reduces stress associated with tight schedules.

Consistency and Routine: Establish a consistent daily routine for walking routes and client visits whenever possible. Predictable schedules benefit both pets and clients by promoting familiarity, reducing anxiety, and ensuring reliable service delivery.

Managing Multiple Clients

Managing multiple clients requires effective organization, clear communication, and proactive planning to deliver exceptional service and maintain client satisfaction. Here's how to manage a diverse client base effectively:

Client Profiles: Maintain detailed client profiles containing essential information, such as pet preferences, medical history, emergency contacts, and scheduling preferences. Update client profiles regularly to reflect any changes or new instructions.

Communication: Establish open lines of communication with clients through phone calls, text messages, or email. Confirm appointment times, share updates on pet behavior or health, and address client inquiries promptly to build trust and rapport.

Appointment Reminders: Send appointment reminders to clients in advance to confirm scheduled walks and reduce no-shows or last-minute cancellations. Use automated reminders via email or text messaging to streamline communication.

Flexible Scheduling: Offer flexible scheduling options to accommodate varying client needs and preferences. Provide early morning, midday, and evening walks to accommodate clients with different work schedules or pet care requirements.

Client Preferences: Respect and accommodate client preferences regarding pet care routines, leash handling techniques, and interaction with other pets or pedestrians during walks. Personalize your services to meet individual client expectations and pet care preferences.

Utilizing Scheduling Software

Scheduling software offers tools and features to streamline appointment management, optimize scheduling efficiency, and enhance client communication in your dog walking business. Here's how to leverage scheduling software effectively:

Features and Benefits: Choose scheduling software that offers features such as calendar integration, appointment scheduling, client management, automated reminders, and customizable settings. Evaluate software options based on your business needs and budget.

Automated Scheduling: Automate appointment scheduling and reminders to save time and minimize scheduling errors. Allow clients to book appointments online, view available time slots, and receive instant confirmation notifications.

Calendar Sync: Sync scheduling software with your digital calendar to manage appointments, availability, and personal commitments in one centralized location. Ensure updates and changes to your schedule are reflected across all synchronized platforms.

Client Accessibility: Provide clients with access to a client portal or mobile app where they can schedule appointments, update pet care instructions, view appointment history, and communicate directly with you. Enhance client satisfaction and convenience through user-friendly interfaces.

Reporting and Analytics: Use reporting tools within scheduling software to track appointment trends, client retention rates, and business performance metrics. Analyze data to identify opportunities for growth, optimize service offerings, and improve operational efficiency.

Training and Support: Take advantage of training resources, tutorials, and customer support provided by scheduling software providers. Familiarize yourself with software features and capabilities to maximize efficiency and leverage advanced functionalities.

Conclusion

Effective scheduling and time management are essential components of running a successful dog walking business. By creating an efficient schedule, managing multiple clients with personalized care, and utilizing scheduling software to streamline operations, you can optimize productivity, enhance client satisfaction, and achieve business growth. Maintain clear communication with clients, prioritize pet care needs, and adapt scheduling practices to meet evolving client preferences and business demands. Continuously evaluate and refine your scheduling strategies to improve efficiency, minimize scheduling conflicts, and deliver exceptional pet care services that exceed client expectations. With strategic planning and proactive scheduling practices, you can establish a reputation for reliability, professionalism, and quality service in the competitive dog walking industry.

Chapter 15: Hiring Employees or Contractors

Deciding When to Hire Help

As your dog walking business grows, the decision to hire employees or contractors becomes crucial for scaling operations, meeting client demand, and expanding service offerings. Here's how to determine when to hire help:

Assess Workload: Evaluate your current workload and client base to identify if existing resources (including yourself) can efficiently manage client requests and daily operations. Signs that you may need additional help include scheduling conflicts, increased client inquiries, or difficulty meeting service demand.

Business Growth: Consider your business growth trajectory and long-term goals. Hiring help can support expansion efforts, enhance service delivery, and free up time for business development activities, such as marketing, client outreach, and strategic planning.

Client Satisfaction: Monitor client feedback and satisfaction levels. If clients express satisfaction with your services but request additional availability or specialized pet care options, hiring help can enable you to meet these requests and enhance overall client experience.

Personal Capacity: Assess your own capacity and availability to manage daily operations, client relationships, and administrative tasks effectively. Hiring help allows you to delegate responsibilities, reduce workload stress, and maintain work-life balance.

Financial Viability: Evaluate your financial position and budget to determine if hiring employees or contractors is financially feasible. Consider projected revenue, anticipated expenses (including payroll costs), and potential return on investment from expanding your service capacity.

Finding and Interviewing Candidates

When searching for candidates to join your dog walking business, prioritize individuals who demonstrate reliability, pet care expertise, and a commitment to exceptional customer service. Here's how to find and interview suitable candidates:

Job Posting: Create a detailed job posting outlining job responsibilities, qualifications (e.g., experience with pet care, availability), and desired skills (e.g., communication, time management). Post job listings on online job boards, social media platforms, local community groups, and pet care websites.

Referrals and Networking: Seek referrals from trusted sources, such as industry peers, pet owners, or local pet-related businesses (e.g., veterinary clinics, pet stores). Networking within professional associations or attending pet care events can also help you connect with potential candidates.

Screening Resumes: Review resumes or applications to identify candidates with relevant experience in dog walking, pet care, or customer service roles. Look for certifications (e.g., pet first aid, dog training), positive client testimonials, and a genuine passion for working with animals.

Conduct Interviews: Schedule interviews with promising candidates to assess their qualifications, personality fit, and alignment with your business values. Prepare interview questions that explore their pet care experience, handling techniques, availability, and willingness to adhere to company policies.

Behavioral Assessments: Consider conducting behavioral assessments or practical skills tests during the interview process to evaluate candidates' ability to handle pets, respond to hypothetical scenarios, and demonstrate professionalism in client interactions.

Background Checks: Conduct background checks, including criminal history and reference verification, to ensure candidates meet your business's safety standards and ethical guidelines for working with pets and clients.

Training and Managing Employees

Once hired, providing comprehensive training and ongoing support is essential for integrating new employees into your dog walking business and maintaining service excellence. Here's how to effectively train and manage employees:

Orientation and Onboarding: Conduct a thorough orientation session to introduce new employees to your business policies, safety protocols, client expectations, and service standards. Provide an overview of daily operations, scheduling procedures, and communication channels.

Pet Care Training: Offer hands-on training in pet care techniques, leash handling, pet behavior management, and emergency procedures (e.g., pet first aid). Demonstrate proper pet interaction techniques and reinforce the importance of providing compassionate care to clients' pets.

Client Relationship Management: Train employees on effective client communication, including how to greet clients professionally, obtain pet care instructions, address client concerns, and maintain positive client relationships. Emphasize the significance of client confidentiality and trust.

Safety and Risk Management: Educate employees on safety precautions during dog walks, including traffic awareness, leash safety, and handling techniques for different pet personalities and behavioral traits. Discuss strategies for managing emergencies or unexpected incidents while ensuring pet and personal safety.

Performance Feedback: Provide regular feedback and performance evaluations to employees to acknowledge strengths, identify areas for improvement, and align performance with business goals. Offer constructive guidance, recognize achievements, and address any performance concerns promptly.

Team Collaboration: Foster a collaborative team environment where employees can share insights, support each other, and collaborate on pet care strategies or client solutions. Encourage open communication, respect for diversity, and a shared commitment to delivering exceptional service.

Conclusion

Hiring employees or contractors for your dog walking business is a significant step toward expanding your service capacity, enhancing client satisfaction, and achieving business growth. By strategically assessing workload demands, recruiting qualified candidates, and providing thorough training and ongoing support, you can build a skilled team capable of delivering reliable pet care services and upholding your business's reputation for excellence. Invest in employee development, foster a positive work culture, and prioritize client satisfaction to sustain long-term success and profitability in the competitive pet care industry. With dedicated team members who share your passion for pet welfare and customer service, your dog walking business can thrive and continue to meet the evolving needs of pet owners in your community.

Chapter 16: Ensuring Dog Safety

Ensuring the safety and well-being of dogs under your care is paramount for running a successful and trusted dog walking business. This chapter covers essential skills, understanding dog behavior, and handling emergencies to safeguard dogs during walks.

Basic Dog Handling Skills

Mastering basic dog handling skills is foundational for providing safe and enjoyable walks for dogs of all breeds and temperaments. Here are key skills to develop:

Leash Handling: Use a sturdy leash of appropriate length and material for controlling dogs effectively. Maintain a firm grip on the leash, keeping it slack to allow freedom of movement without excessive tension.

Approaching Dogs: Approach dogs calmly and avoid sudden movements or loud noises that may startle them. Allow dogs to approach you first if they are hesitant, using a relaxed posture and gentle voice to establish trust.

Body Language Interpretation: Learn to interpret dog body language to gauge their mood, intentions, and comfort level. Signs of agitation, fear, or aggression include raised hackles, bared teeth, growling, or defensive postures.

Handling Techniques: Use gentle handling techniques to guide dogs on walks, avoiding jerky movements or harsh corrections. Use positive reinforcement (e.g., treats, praise) to encourage desired behaviors such as walking calmly on leash.

Safe Restraint: Practice safe restraint techniques when encountering other dogs, pedestrians, or potential distractions during walks. Maintain control of the leash and redirect attention as needed to prevent conflicts or accidents.

Understanding Dog Behavior

Understanding dog behavior enhances your ability to anticipate reactions, address concerns proactively, and build positive relationships with dogs in your care. Consider the following aspects of dog behavior:

Socialization Needs: Recognize the importance of socialization for dogs to interact positively with other pets, people, and environments. Encourage positive social experiences during walks to promote confidence and reduce anxiety.

Body Language Cues: Interpret body language cues such as tail wagging, ear position, eye contact, and vocalizations to understand dogs' emotions and intentions. Respond appropriately to signals of comfort, stress, or discomfort.

Behavioral Triggers: Identify common behavioral triggers that may cause dogs to react negatively, such as unfamiliar surroundings, loud noises, or encounters with aggressive dogs. Take preventive measures to minimize stress and ensure a calm walking experience.

Exercise Requirements: Tailor walking routines to meet each dog's exercise needs based on breed, age, health, and energy level. Provide adequate opportunities for physical activity, mental stimulation, and bathroom breaks during walks.

Bonding Opportunities: Use walks as bonding opportunities to strengthen your relationship with dogs through positive interactions, playtime, and attentive care. Build trust and rapport by respecting individual preferences and reinforcing desired behaviors.

Dealing with Emergencies

Preparedness for emergencies is essential for handling unexpected situations and ensuring the safety of dogs in your care. Equip yourself with the knowledge and skills to respond effectively to emergencies:

First Aid Training: Obtain training in pet first aid and CPR from reputable organizations to administer immediate care in case of injuries, choking incidents, or medical emergencies during walks. Carry a pet first aid kit containing essentials such as bandages, antiseptic wipes, and emergency contact information.

Emergency Response Protocols: Establish protocols for responding to emergencies, including contact information for veterinary clinics, emergency hotlines, and pet owners. Remain calm, assess the situation, and prioritize the safety and well-being of the dog while seeking prompt veterinary assistance if needed.

Heat and Cold Safety: Protect dogs from extreme temperatures by adjusting walking schedules during hot weather, providing access to shade and water, and avoiding hot pavement that can burn paw pads. Use protective gear such as dog booties or coats in cold weather to prevent hypothermia.

Encounter with Wildlife: Be vigilant for encounters with wildlife (e.g., snakes, aggressive animals) during walks in natural settings. Maintain control of dogs on leash, avoid areas with known wildlife activity, and seek veterinary advice if a dog shows signs of injury or exposure to wildlife hazards.

Lost Dog Protocol: Prepare a protocol for handling lost dogs, including steps to search nearby areas, notify pet owners immediately, and contact local animal shelters or authorities for assistance in locating and safely returning the dog.

Conclusion

Ensuring dog safety is fundamental to the ethical practice and reputation of your dog walking business. By mastering basic handling skills, understanding dog behavior, and preparing for emergencies, you create a safe and enriching environment for dogs during walks. Prioritize ongoing education, training, and professional development to enhance your expertise in pet care and emergency response techniques. Build trusting relationships with pet owners by demonstrating a commitment to the safety, well-being, and happiness of their beloved pets. Your dedication to dog safety not only fosters client loyalty and satisfaction but also promotes the long-term success and credibility of your dog walking business in the competitive pet care industry.

Chapter 17: Providing Excellent Customer Service

Delivering excellent customer service is essential for building a loyal client base, fostering positive relationships, and growing your dog walking business. This chapter explores effective communication with clients, handling complaints, and strategies for exceeding client expectations.

Communicating Effectively with Clients

Effective communication forms the foundation of exceptional customer service in your dog walking business. Build trust, clarity, and rapport with clients through the following practices:

Initial Consultations: Conduct thorough initial consultations with new clients to discuss pet care preferences, walking schedules, health considerations, and emergency contacts. Listen attentively to client expectations and gather detailed information to personalize service delivery.

Clear Communication Channels: Establish clear communication channels, including phone calls, text messages, email, or a client portal, to facilitate prompt and responsive communication. Use preferred communication methods identified by clients to ensure accessibility and convenience.

Appointment Confirmations: Confirm scheduled appointments with clients in advance through automated reminders, personalized messages, or confirmation calls. Confirm details such as appointment time, meeting location, and any special instructions for pet care.

Regular Updates: Provide regular updates to clients during dog walks, including photos, videos, or written summaries of their pet's activities and behavior. Share highlights of the walk, milestones achieved, and any observations relevant to pet care.

Transparency: Maintain transparency in your interactions with clients regarding service fees, scheduling policies, and changes to service availability. Address client inquiries or concerns promptly and offer clear explanations or resolutions as needed.

Handling Complaints and Issues

Resolving client complaints and addressing issues promptly demonstrates your commitment to customer satisfaction and service excellence. Follow these steps to handle complaints effectively:

Active Listening: Listen actively to client concerns without interruption, allowing them to express their dissatisfaction or issues fully. Validate their feelings and acknowledge the impact of the situation on their experience.

Empathy and Understanding: Demonstrate empathy by putting yourself in the client's position and understanding their perspective. Show genuine concern for their feelings, pet's well-being, and the importance of resolving the issue to their satisfaction.

Problem Resolution: Take proactive steps to address the issue or complaint promptly. Gather relevant information, investigate the root cause of the problem, and propose solutions or corrective actions that align with client expectations.

Open Communication: Maintain open lines of communication throughout the resolution process. Keep clients informed of progress, updates, or any additional steps taken to rectify the situation and prevent recurrence.

Apology and Accountability: If your dog walking business is at fault, apologize sincerely for any inconvenience or misunderstanding caused. Accept accountability for mistakes, errors in service delivery, or miscommunication and strive to regain client trust through corrective actions.

Going Above and Beyond for Client Satisfaction

Differentiate your dog walking business by exceeding client expectations and delivering memorable experiences that inspire loyalty and positive word-of-mouth referrals:

Personalized Service: Personalize your services based on client preferences, pet care needs, and individual pet personalities. Offer customized walking routes, playtime activities, or additional services (e.g., pet grooming, feeding) to enhance client satisfaction.

Anticipate Client Needs: Anticipate client needs and proactively offer solutions or recommendations that enhance their pet care experience. Provide insights on pet health, behavior tips, or local pet-friendly activities that align with their interests.

Surprise and Delight: Surprise clients with unexpected gestures of appreciation, such as birthday greetings for pets, holiday-themed treats, or personalized thank-you notes. Demonstrate your thoughtfulness and commitment to their pet's well-being.

Feedback and Reviews: Encourage clients to provide feedback and testimonials about their experience with your dog walking services. Use positive reviews to showcase client satisfaction and build credibility for potential clients seeking reliable pet care services.

Follow-Up and Long-Term Relationships: Follow up with clients after services to inquire about their satisfaction, address any lingering concerns, and express appreciation for their trust in your business. Nurture long-term relationships through consistent, reliable service and genuine care for their pets.

Conclusion

Providing excellent customer service is a cornerstone of success in the dog walking industry, fostering client loyalty, and generating positive referrals. By communicating effectively, resolving issues with empathy and accountability, and exceeding client expectations through personalized care and thoughtful gestures, you can differentiate your dog walking business and build a reputation for excellence. Continuously seek client feedback, adapt to evolving client preferences, and uphold high standards of service delivery to sustain long-term relationships and business growth. Your commitment to exceptional customer service not only enhances client satisfaction but also strengthens the foundation of trust and reliability that defines your dog walking business in the competitive marketplace.

Chapter 18: Growing Your Business

Growing your dog walking business involves strategic planning, expansion of services, and scaling operations to meet increasing client demand. This chapter explores key strategies for expanding your service area, offering additional services, and scaling your business effectively.

Expanding Your Service Area

Expanding your service area allows you to reach a broader clientele and increase your business's visibility in new neighborhoods or communities. Consider the following steps to expand your service area:

Market Research: Conduct market research to identify neighborhoods or regions with a high concentration of potential clients who require dog walking services. Analyze demographic trends, pet ownership rates, and competitor presence in target areas.

Assess Logistics: Evaluate logistics such as travel time, transportation costs, and operational feasibility of servicing new locations. Determine optimal routes, scheduling flexibility, and resource allocation to ensure efficient service delivery.

Marketing Strategies: Develop targeted marketing strategies to promote your services in new service areas. Use digital marketing tactics, local advertising channels, and community outreach events to raise awareness, attract new clients, and establish a presence in target neighborhoods.

Client Referrals: Leverage existing client relationships and positive word-of-mouth referrals to expand your client base into new geographical areas. Encourage satisfied clients to recommend your services to friends, family, and colleagues living in nearby neighborhoods.

Networking: Join local business associations, pet-related organizations, or community groups in target areas to network with potential clients and build relationships with local influencers. Participate in local events, sponsor pet-friendly activities, or collaborate with neighborhood businesses to increase visibility.

Offering Additional Services (Pet Sitting, Training)

Diversifying your service offerings enhances your business's value proposition, attracts new clients, and increases revenue streams. Consider expanding into the following additional services:

Pet Sitting: Offer pet sitting services to clients who require overnight care, extended absence pet care, or personalized in-home visits. Provide companionship, feeding, exercise, and basic grooming services tailored to each pet's routine and preferences.

Behavioral Training: Partner with certified dog trainers or obtain training certifications yourself to offer basic obedience training, leash manners, or behavioral modification sessions. Help clients address common behavioral issues, improve pet-owner communication, and strengthen the human-animal bond.

Grooming Services: Collaborate with local groomers or invest in basic grooming equipment to offer grooming services such as brushing, nail trimming, ear cleaning, and coat conditioning during dog walking appointments or standalone grooming sessions.

Pet Transport: Provide safe and reliable pet transportation services for clients who require pet transport to veterinary appointments, grooming salons, or pet daycare facilities. Ensure pets travel comfortably, securely, and in compliance with local transportation regulations.

Specialized Care: Introduce specialized care services for senior pets, puppies, or pets with medical needs, including administering medications, monitoring health conditions, and accommodating dietary restrictions or mobility challenges.

Scaling Your Business

Scaling your dog walking business involves expanding operational capacity, optimizing workflows, and maintaining service quality as demand increases. Implement scalable growth strategies to support business expansion:

Operational Efficiency: Streamline operational processes, such as scheduling, client communication, and administrative tasks, using technology tools and software. Automate routine tasks, optimize route planning, and centralize client management to improve efficiency.

Staffing Solutions: Hire additional staff or contractors to meet growing demand while maintaining service quality and client satisfaction. Implement training programs, standardized procedures, and performance metrics to ensure consistency in service delivery.

Infrastructure Investment: Invest in infrastructure improvements, such as fleet vehicles, equipment upgrades, or office space expansion, to support increased service capacity and operational scalability.

Client Retention: Focus on client retention strategies, such as loyalty programs, referral incentives, and personalized client interactions, to nurture long-term relationships and sustain business growth. Monitor client satisfaction levels, address feedback promptly, and adapt services based on client preferences.

Financial Planning: Develop a financial plan that includes budgeting for growth, forecasting revenue projections, and managing expenses associated with scaling operations. Seek guidance from financial advisors or business consultants to optimize financial performance and mitigate risks associated with business expansion.

Conclusion

Growing your dog walking business requires strategic planning, innovation, and a commitment to delivering exceptional pet care services. By expanding your service area, offering additional services, and scaling operations effectively, you can attract new clients, increase revenue streams, and establish a strong market presence in the competitive pet care industry. Continuously assess market opportunities, adapt to changing client needs, and invest in business development initiatives that support sustainable growth and long-term success. With a focus on quality service delivery, client satisfaction, and operational excellence, your dog walking business can thrive and evolve to meet the evolving demands of pet owners seeking reliable and trusted pet care providers.

Chapter 19: Utilizing Technology

In today's digital age, leveraging technology is essential for optimizing efficiency, enhancing client experience, and streamlining operations in your dog walking business. This chapter explores the benefits of using software, apps, GPS tracking, and online management tools to innovate your services and foster growth.

Software and Apps for Dog Walkers

Choosing the right software and mobile apps can revolutionize how you manage appointments, communicate with clients, and streamline daily operations:

Appointment Scheduling: Utilize scheduling software to manage client appointments efficiently. Offer clients the convenience of booking services online, viewing availability in real-time, and receiving automated appointment reminders.

Client Management: Centralize client information, pet care preferences, and scheduling history in a secure database. Use client management software to maintain detailed records, track client interactions, and personalize service delivery based on individual pet needs.

Mobile Apps: Adopt mobile apps designed for dog walkers to access essential features on the go. Use apps for GPS navigation, client communication, pet care instructions, and capturing real-time updates during walks, such as photos or activity reports.

Payment Processing: Integrate payment processing solutions into your software to accept secure online payments, automate invoicing, and track financial transactions seamlessly. Provide clients with flexible payment options, such as credit card payments or recurring billing for ongoing services.

GPS Tracking for Client Peace of Mind

Implementing GPS tracking technology enhances transparency, security, and peace of mind for clients entrusting their pets to your care:

Real-Time Updates: Use GPS tracking devices or mobile app features to provide clients with real-time updates on their pet's location, route taken during walks, and duration of each session. Ensure transparency and accountability by sharing location-based notifications or activity summaries.

Safety Assurance: Demonstrate your commitment to pet safety by monitoring walking routes, ensuring pets remain within designated safe zones, and promptly addressing any deviations or unexpected incidents during walks. Use GPS tracking data to respond proactively to emergencies or client inquiries.

Client Communication: Incorporate GPS tracking insights into client communication to reassure pet owners of their pet's well-being, adherence to scheduled appointments, and adherence to specified walking routes. Use visual maps or location updates to illustrate the quality and reliability of your services.

Emergency Preparedness: Leverage GPS tracking technology to facilitate swift response times in case of emergencies, such as lost pets, unexpected delays, or client-requested changes to walking schedules. Coordinate with clients, emergency contacts, or local authorities as needed to ensure pet safety and client satisfaction.

Managing Bookings and Payments Online

Transitioning to online booking and payment systems enhances convenience, accessibility, and operational efficiency for your dog walking business:

User-Friendly Platforms: Offer clients user-friendly online portals or booking platforms to browse service offerings, check availability, and schedule appointments with ease.

Customize booking forms to capture essential client information, pet care preferences, and special instructions.

Automated Reminders: Send automated appointment reminders via email or SMS to clients to confirm scheduled appointments, provide service details, and prompt timely responses to booking inquiries. Reduce no-show rates and optimize scheduling efficiency with automated reminder notifications.

Secure Payment Gateways: Integrate secure payment gateways into your website or booking platform to facilitate seamless online payments. Accept major credit cards, electronic transfers, or digital wallet payments to accommodate client preferences and streamline financial transactions.

Booking Flexibility: Offer flexible booking options, such as recurring appointments, last-minute scheduling, or customizable service packages, to cater to diverse client needs and pet care schedules. Use online booking systems to accommodate client preferences for service duration, frequency, and additional service requests.

Conclusion

Utilizing technology effectively in your dog walking business enhances operational efficiency, improves client satisfaction, and strengthens your competitive advantage in the pet care industry. By adopting software and mobile apps for scheduling, implementing GPS tracking for transparency and safety, and managing bookings and payments online, you can streamline service delivery, optimize resource management, and elevate the overall client experience. Embrace innovation, stay informed about technological advancements, and adapt your business strategies to leverage technology solutions that align with your business goals and client expectations. With a commitment to integrating technology into your daily operations, your dog walking business can thrive, grow, and continue to exceed client expectations while setting new standards for excellence in pet care services.

Chapter 20: Social Media and Online Presence

Establishing a strong social media presence and leveraging online platforms is crucial for promoting your dog walking business, connecting with clients, and building a reputable brand. This chapter explores effective strategies for creating engaging content, building a following on social media, and utilizing online reviews and testimonials to enhance visibility and client trust.

Creating Engaging Content

Creating compelling and relevant content on social media platforms is essential for capturing audience attention, showcasing your expertise, and promoting your dog walking services:

Visual Storytelling: Share captivating photos and videos of happy dogs on walks, playful moments, and client interactions. Highlight scenic routes, pet-friendly locations, and seasonal activities to engage followers and evoke emotional connections.

Educational Content: Provide valuable pet care tips, training advice, and behavioral insights to educate pet owners and demonstrate your knowledge in the dog walking industry. Address common concerns, share practical solutions, and establish yourself as a trusted authority.

Client Testimonials: Feature client testimonials, success stories, and positive feedback to build credibility and reassure potential clients of your exceptional service quality. Use quotes, case studies, or video testimonials to highlight satisfied clients and their pets' positive experiences.

Behind-the-Scenes: Offer behind-the-scenes glimpses of your daily operations, team members, or community involvement. Showcase your passion for pet care, dedication to client satisfaction, and the personal touch that sets your business apart.

Interactive Content: Encourage audience engagement through polls, quizzes, contests, or interactive Q&A sessions. Solicit feedback, respond to inquiries promptly, and foster meaningful conversations with followers to strengthen relationships and increase brand loyalty.

Building a Following on Social Media

Building a loyal and engaged following on social media requires strategic planning, consistent engagement, and authenticity in your interactions:

Platform Selection: Identify social media platforms (e.g., Instagram, Facebook, Twitter) that resonate most with your target audience and align with your business objectives.

Focus your efforts on platforms where pet owners are active and receptive to pet-related content.

Content Calendar: Develop a content calendar to plan and schedule posts, ensuring regular and timely updates that maintain audience interest. Incorporate themed campaigns, seasonal promotions, or trending topics to diversify content and attract new followers.

Hashtag Strategy: Research and use relevant hashtags to increase the visibility of your posts and attract followers interested in pet care, dog walking services, and related topics. Create branded hashtags or participate in trending hashtags to expand your reach and foster community engagement.

Cross-Promotion: Collaborate with local businesses, pet influencers, or community organizations to cross-promote content and reach a broader audience. Partner with complementary brands or participate in collaborative campaigns to leverage mutual networks and increase social media exposure.

Consistent Brand Voice: Maintain a consistent brand voice, tone, and visual style across all social media platforms. Reflect your business values, personality, and commitment to exceptional pet care in every interaction to build brand recognition and trust among followers.

Utilizing Online Reviews and Testimonials

Harness the power of online reviews and testimonials to build credibility, attract new clients, and showcase your dog walking business's reputation for excellence:

Review Platforms: Encourage satisfied clients to leave reviews on popular review platforms such as Google My Business, Yelp, or Facebook. Monitor reviews regularly, respond promptly to feedback (both positive and constructive), and demonstrate your commitment to client satisfaction.

Testimonial Showcase: Display client testimonials prominently on your website, social media profiles, or promotional materials. Use testimonials to highlight specific benefits, personalized experiences, and positive outcomes that clients have experienced with your dog walking services.

Case Studies: Develop detailed case studies or success stories that illustrate your expertise, problem-solving abilities, and the positive impact of your services on pets and their owners. Showcase before-and-after scenarios, client testimonials, and measurable results to reinforce credibility and trust.

Referral Program: Implement a referral program that rewards clients for referring new customers to your dog walking services. Encourage word-of-mouth referrals, incentivize client advocacy, and capitalize on positive experiences shared within personal networks and online communities.

Social Proof: Leverage social proof, such as awards, certifications, or industry recognition, to validate your business's credibility and expertise in the dog walking industry. Highlight affiliations with reputable organizations, participation in community events, or positive media coverage to enhance your online reputation.

Conclusion

Creating a vibrant social media presence and leveraging online platforms effectively are indispensable strategies for growing your dog walking business, enhancing client engagement, and building a trusted brand reputation. By creating engaging content that resonates with pet owners, building a loyal following through consistent interaction and authenticity, and harnessing the influence of online reviews and testimonials, you can elevate your business visibility, attract new clients, and foster long-term client loyalty. Embrace creativity, stay responsive to client feedback, and adapt your social media strategies to reflect evolving trends and client preferences in the dynamic pet care industry. With a strategic approach to social media and online presence, your dog walking business can thrive and continue to make a positive impact on pets and their owners in your community.

Chapter 21: Handling Difficult Dogs and Situations

Navigating challenging situations with dogs requires patience, skill, and a deep understanding of canine behavior. This chapter explores effective techniques for handling aggressive dogs, managing multiple dogs at once, and dealing with unforeseen circumstances to ensure the safety and well-being of both pets and dog walkers.

Techniques for Handling Aggressive Dogs

Encountering aggression in dogs during walks can be unsettling, but employing the right techniques can help diffuse tense situations and ensure safety:

Assessment and Observation: Assess the dog's body language, vocalizations, and environmental triggers to gauge the level of aggression and potential causes. Remain calm, maintain a safe distance, and avoid sudden movements to prevent escalating the dog's aggression.

Maintain Control: Use a firm, yet calm demeanor to assert control over the situation. Avoid direct eye contact or confrontational postures that may provoke further aggression. Position yourself sideways to the dog and maintain a neutral stance to reduce perceived threat.

Redirect Attention: Distract the dog's focus away from the perceived threat or trigger by using positive reinforcement techniques, such as offering treats, engaging in play, or redirecting their attention to a familiar command or toy. Redirecting their focus can help de-escalate tension and encourage more positive behavior.

Create Distance: If safe to do so, create distance between yourself and the aggressive dog by calmly moving away or seeking a physical barrier (e.g., a parked car, fence). Avoid turning your back on the dog abruptly, as sudden movements may provoke chase behavior.

Seek Professional Help: For severe cases of aggression or unpredictable behavior, seek assistance from professional dog trainers, behaviorists, or animal control authorities. Collaborate with the dog's owner to address underlying causes and implement behavior modification strategies to improve the dog's response to walking situations.

Managing Multiple Dogs at Once

Walking multiple dogs simultaneously requires careful planning, effective management strategies, and a focus on maintaining control and safety:

Pre-Walk Assessment: Evaluate each dog's temperament, behavior around other dogs, and obedience level before initiating a group walk. Select dogs with compatible personalities and similar walking paces to minimize potential conflicts or disruptions.

Establish Pack Order: Establish a clear pack order and leadership role by positioning yourself as the pack leader. Use consistent commands, leash handling techniques, and reward-based training to reinforce positive behavior and maintain order during group walks.

Separate Leashes: Use individual leashes for each dog to maintain control and prevent tangling or leash-related incidents. Choose sturdy, non-retractable leashes of appropriate length and strength to accommodate the size and strength of each dog.

Monitor Interactions: Stay vigilant and monitor interactions between dogs throughout the walk. Anticipate potential triggers or signs of tension, such as body language changes, vocalizations, or competitive behavior over resources (e.g., food, territory).

Divide Attention: Allocate equal attention to each dog to ensure their needs are met during the walk. Rotate walking positions, offer praise and rewards for good behavior, and intervene promptly to address conflicts or disruptive behaviors before they escalate.

Dealing with Unforeseen Circumstances

Unforeseen circumstances, such as weather changes, medical emergencies, or unexpected encounters, require quick thinking and adaptability to ensure the safety and well-being of dogs under your care:

Emergency Preparedness: Carry a well-equipped first aid kit, emergency contact information for each dog's owner, and essential supplies (e.g., water, treats) during walks. Familiarize yourself with basic pet first aid techniques, such as CPR and wound care, to respond effectively in emergencies.

Weather Awareness: Monitor weather forecasts and adjust walking schedules or routes accordingly to protect dogs from extreme heat, cold, or inclement weather conditions. Provide access to shaded areas, fresh water, and protective gear (e.g., dog boots, coats) as needed to maintain comfort and safety.

Safety Protocols: Implement safety protocols for navigating busy streets, encountering wildlife, or approaching unfamiliar dogs during walks. Maintain situational awareness, use reflective clothing or accessories for visibility, and adhere to local leash laws and regulations to prevent accidents or incidents.

Client Communication: Keep clients informed of any unexpected incidents, changes in walking conditions, or concerns regarding their pet's well-being. Maintain open lines of communication, provide timely updates, and collaborate with clients to address emergencies or unforeseen circumstances promptly.

Continued Education: Stay informed about best practices in dog handling, behavior modification techniques, and emergency response protocols through ongoing education, professional development opportunities, and networking with fellow pet care professionals. Enhance your skills and confidence in managing diverse situations to ensure the safety and satisfaction of both dogs and their owners.

Conclusion

Handling difficult dogs and navigating challenging situations during dog walks requires a combination of knowledge, skill, and a proactive approach to ensuring safety and positive experiences for all involved. By employing effective techniques for handling aggression, managing multiple dogs, and responding to unforeseen circumstances with composure and readiness, you can uphold high standards of care, build client trust, and establish your reputation as a reliable and skilled dog walking professional. Continuously refine your handling skills, stay prepared for emergencies, and prioritize the well-being of dogs under your care to maintain a successful and rewarding career in the pet care industry.

Chapter 22: Health and Wellness for Dogs

Ensuring the health and well-being of dogs in your care is paramount as a dog walking professional. This chapter explores essential aspects of canine health, recognizing signs of illness or injury, and providing effective first aid to promote the safety and happiness of the dogs you walk.

Understanding Basic Canine Health

Understanding the fundamentals of canine health equips you with the knowledge to recognize signs of wellness and detect potential health issues:

Physical Wellness: Monitor dogs for signs of physical health, including a healthy weight, clear eyes, clean ears, and a shiny coat. Regularly assess their mobility, energy levels, and appetite to gauge overall well-being.

Nutritional Needs: Provide balanced nutrition and access to fresh water during walks. Familiarize yourself with dietary requirements specific to each dog's breed, age, and health condition. Discuss dietary preferences or restrictions with owners to ensure consistency in feeding practices.

Exercise Requirements: Tailor exercise routines to meet each dog's age, breed characteristics, and fitness level. Incorporate opportunities for mental stimulation, play, and social interaction to promote physical fitness and mental well-being during walks.

Hygiene and Grooming: Maintain good hygiene practices, such as regular grooming, nail trimming, and dental care, to support overall health and prevent common issues like mats, infections, or dental problems. Use appropriate grooming tools and techniques suitable for each dog's coat type and grooming preferences.

Vaccination and Preventive Care: Verify that dogs are up-to-date on vaccinations, parasite prevention (e.g., flea, tick, heartworm), and routine veterinary check-ups. Communicate with owners about preventive care schedules and any specific health concerns or medical conditions requiring attention.

Recognizing Signs of Illness or Injury

Recognizing signs of illness or injury during walks enables prompt intervention and appropriate care for dogs in distress:

Behavioral Changes: Monitor changes in behavior, such as lethargy, excessive panting, reluctance to walk, or unusual aggression. Note deviations from normal behavior patterns and investigate potential causes, including environmental stressors or underlying health issues.

Physical Symptoms: Look for physical symptoms indicating illness or injury, such as limping, lameness, excessive scratching, vomiting, diarrhea, or respiratory distress. Conduct a visual inspection for cuts, bruises, swelling, or signs of discomfort that may require immediate attention.

Temperature Regulation: Be mindful of temperature-related stressors, such as heat exhaustion or hypothermia, during extreme weather conditions. Provide access to shade, water, and cooling measures (e.g., wet towels, cooling vests) to prevent overheating and ensure comfort.

Digestive Health: Monitor digestive health by observing stool consistency, frequency of bowel movements, and signs of gastrointestinal distress (e.g., bloating, constipation). Address dietary concerns, food intolerances, or changes in eating habits promptly to maintain digestive wellness.

Urinary Health: Monitor urinary habits, including frequency of urination, changes in urine color or odor, and signs of discomfort during urination. Report any abnormalities to owners and seek veterinary advice for further evaluation and treatment.

Providing First Aid for Dogs

Being prepared to administer first aid effectively can mitigate risks and provide immediate relief in emergencies or unexpected situations:

Emergency Preparedness: Carry a well-stocked first aid kit containing essential supplies, including bandages, gauze pads, antiseptic wipes, adhesive tape, scissors, tweezers, and disposable gloves. Include emergency contact information for veterinarians and pet owners.

Wound Care: Clean and disinfect minor wounds, cuts, or abrasions using sterile saline solution or antiseptic wipes. Apply a protective dressing or bandage to minimize contamination and promote healing. Monitor wound healing progress and seek veterinary attention for severe injuries or infections.

Heat-Related Illness: Recognize signs of heat exhaustion, such as excessive panting, drooling, weakness, or collapse. Move the dog to a cool, shaded area, offer water to drink, and use cool compresses or immerse in cool water to lower body temperature gradually. Seek veterinary care if symptoms persist or worsen.

Choking or Respiratory Distress: Perform abdominal thrusts or chest compressions to dislodge obstructive objects or clear airway obstructions. Administer rescue breathing techniques if necessary and monitor breathing until veterinary assistance is available.

Poisoning or Ingestion: Identify signs of poisoning, including vomiting, diarrhea, drooling, seizures, or behavioral changes. Contact a poison control hotline or seek immediate veterinary care for prompt diagnosis and treatment options.

Conclusion

Promoting health and wellness for dogs during walks requires vigilance, empathy, and a commitment to providing compassionate care. By understanding basic canine health principles, recognizing signs of illness or injury, and being prepared to administer first aid effectively, you can ensure the safety, comfort, and happiness of dogs entrusted to your care. Communicate openly with owners about health concerns, follow preventive care guidelines, and stay informed about emerging health issues or seasonal risks affecting dogs in your community. With a proactive approach to canine health and wellness, you can uphold high standards of care, build trust with clients, and foster a positive reputation as a dedicated dog walking professional committed to enhancing the lives of pets and their owners.

Chapter 23: Legal Considerations and Liability

Navigating legal considerations and understanding liability issues are essential aspects of running a successful dog walking business. This chapter explores key legal considerations, strategies for protecting yourself legally, and the importance of keeping detailed records to ensure compliance and mitigate risks effectively.

Understanding Liability Issues

As a dog walking professional, you assume responsibility for the safety and well-being of the dogs under your care, as well as potential interactions with clients and the public. Understanding liability issues involves:

Duty of Care: Recognize your duty of care to provide a safe environment and exercise reasonable precautions to prevent harm to dogs, clients, and third parties during walks. Uphold industry standards, follow local regulations, and prioritize safety in all aspects of your business operations.

Legal Responsibility: Acknowledge legal responsibilities associated with dog walking, including adherence to local leash laws, animal welfare regulations, and liability for damages caused by dogs under your supervision. Consult legal resources or professional advisors to clarify legal obligations specific to your business location and operations.

Liability Insurance: Obtain comprehensive liability insurance coverage tailored to pet care professionals, including general liability insurance and animal bailee coverage. Insurance policies can safeguard against financial losses, legal expenses, or claims arising from injuries, property damage, or incidents involving dogs in your care.

Contractual Agreements: Implement clear and enforceable contractual agreements with clients, outlining services provided, fees, cancellation policies, and liability limitations. Include waivers of liability clauses to define responsibilities and risks associated with dog walking services, promoting transparency and mutual understanding.

Protecting Yourself Legally

Implement proactive measures to protect yourself legally and minimize potential risks associated with operating a dog walking business:

Business Entity Formation: Consider forming a legal business entity, such as a limited liability company (LLC), to separate personal and business liabilities. LLC status can offer personal asset protection and mitigate financial risks associated with business operations or legal disputes.

Professional Indemnity: Maintain professional standards and ethical conduct in all client interactions to mitigate claims of negligence or misconduct. Uphold confidentiality, respect client privacy, and prioritize the best interests of dogs under your care to uphold professional integrity.

Risk Management Practices: Implement risk management practices, including safety protocols, staff training, and emergency preparedness plans, to minimize potential hazards and enhance operational safety. Conduct regular risk assessments, address potential liabilities proactively, and update policies as needed to reflect evolving industry standards or regulatory requirements.

Legal Compliance: Stay informed about legal obligations, licensing requirements, and regulatory changes affecting pet care businesses in your jurisdiction. Maintain compliance with local, state, and federal laws governing animal welfare, business registration, tax obligations, and health and safety standards applicable to dog walking services.

Keeping Detailed Records

Maintaining accurate and detailed records is essential for demonstrating accountability, tracking business performance, and facilitating effective communication with clients and regulatory authorities:

Client Information: Maintain comprehensive client records, including contact details, emergency contacts, pet profiles, veterinary information, and service preferences. Document client communications, service agreements, and consent forms to ensure clarity and accountability in service delivery.

Daily Logs: Keep detailed daily logs of each dog's walking schedule, activities, behavior observations, and any incidents or concerns encountered during walks. Record weather conditions, route maps, and notable events to provide context and facilitate continuity of care.

Financial Records: Organize financial records, including income statements, expense receipts, invoicing records, and tax filings, to track business finances accurately and facilitate financial planning or reporting requirements. Use accounting software or professional services to streamline record-keeping and ensure compliance with financial regulations.

Incident Reports: Document incidents, accidents, or injuries involving dogs, clients, or third parties promptly and accurately. Record details of the incident, actions taken, witness statements, and communications with affected parties to support insurance claims, legal proceedings, or regulatory inquiries.

Data Security: Implement data security measures to protect client confidentiality, sensitive business information, and digital records from unauthorized access or data breaches. Use secure storage solutions, encryption technologies, and password protection protocols to safeguard electronic records and maintain client trust.

Conclusion

Understanding legal considerations, managing liability risks, and maintaining detailed records are critical aspects of operating a responsible and successful dog walking business. By prioritizing safety, adhering to legal obligations, and implementing robust risk management practices, you can protect yourself legally, enhance client confidence, and foster long-term business sustainability. Stay proactive in legal compliance, seek professional guidance when needed, and uphold ethical standards to uphold your reputation as a trusted and reputable dog walking professional in your community. By maintaining meticulous records, embracing transparency, and addressing potential liabilities proactively, you can navigate legal challenges effectively and focus on delivering exceptional care and service to dogs and their owners with confidence and peace of mind.

Chapter 24: Client Retention Strategies

Building strong, lasting relationships with clients is crucial for the sustained success of your dog walking business. This chapter delves into effective strategies for cultivating client loyalty, rewarding long-term clients, and consistently delivering exceptional service to enhance client satisfaction and retention.

Building Long-Term Relationships with Clients

Creating meaningful connections and fostering trust are foundational to building long-term relationships with clients:

Personalized Approach: Take the time to understand each client's preferences, pet care needs, and expectations. Listen actively, ask questions, and demonstrate genuine interest in their pets to establish rapport and build a personalized service experience.

Effective Communication: Maintain open lines of communication with clients through regular updates, timely responses to inquiries, and proactive outreach. Use multiple communication channels, such as phone calls, emails, or messaging apps, to accommodate client preferences and ensure accessibility.

Consistent Reliability: Prioritize punctuality, reliability, and consistency in service delivery to build confidence and trust with clients. Adhere to scheduled appointments, follow established routines, and notify clients promptly of any changes or unforeseen circumstances affecting their pet's care.

Professionalism and Integrity: Uphold professional standards, ethical conduct, and transparency in all client interactions. Demonstrate integrity, respect client confidentiality, and prioritize the well-being of pets to foster trust and maintain a positive reputation as a dependable pet care provider.

Rewarding Loyal Clients

Acknowledging and appreciating client loyalty encourages repeat business and strengthens client relationships:

Loyalty Programs: Implement loyalty programs or rewards initiatives to incentivize repeat business and express appreciation for client loyalty. Offer discounts, promotional offers, or exclusive perks for recurring clients or referrals to demonstrate value and encourage continued engagement.

Special Offers and Discounts: Extend special offers, seasonal promotions, or discounted service packages to loyal clients as a gesture of appreciation. Tailor incentives to align with client preferences, pet care needs, and budget considerations to enhance perceived value and encourage repeat bookings.

Personalized Recognition: Celebrate milestones, such as anniversaries or special occasions, with personalized messages, handwritten notes, or small tokens of appreciation. Recognize client loyalty through personalized gestures that demonstrate gratitude and strengthen emotional connections with clients.

Feedback and Engagement: Seek client feedback through surveys, reviews, or informal conversations to gauge satisfaction levels, identify areas for improvement, and tailor services to meet evolving client expectations. Actively engage with client feedback, implement suggestions for enhancement, and demonstrate responsiveness to client input.

Consistently Providing High-Quality Service

Delivering exceptional service consistently reinforces client satisfaction and loyalty:

Customized Pet Care Plans: Develop customized pet care plans tailored to each dog's unique needs, preferences, and behavioral characteristics. Collaborate with clients to establish clear expectations, preferences for care routines, and proactive strategies to enhance pet comfort and well-being during walks.

Quality Assurance: Maintain rigorous quality standards, adhere to best practices in pet care, and prioritize safety measures to ensure optimal service delivery. Conduct regular assessments, monitor service quality, and implement continuous improvement initiatives to uphold high standards of excellence.

Professional Development: Invest in ongoing training, certification programs, or professional development opportunities to enhance skills, expand knowledge of pet care best practices, and stay abreast of industry trends. Embrace lifelong learning to refine expertise, enrich service offerings, and provide value-added solutions to clients.

Timely Follow-Up: Follow up with clients after service appointments to gather feedback, address any concerns promptly, and reinforce client satisfaction. Demonstrate responsiveness, attentiveness to pet care needs, and commitment to exceeding client expectations to foster loyalty and retention.

Conclusion

Client retention strategies are integral to sustaining a thriving dog walking business and fostering enduring relationships with clients. By prioritizing personalized client interactions, rewarding loyalty, and consistently delivering high-quality service, you can cultivate trust, enhance client satisfaction, and differentiate your business in a competitive market. Embrace client feedback, adapt service offerings to meet evolving needs, and celebrate client milestones to strengthen emotional connections and promote long-term loyalty. By investing in client relationships, demonstrating professionalism, and exceeding expectations with each interaction, you can build a loyal client base, drive business growth, and position your dog walking business for sustained success in the pet care industry.

Chapter 25: Seasonal Considerations

Adapting your dog walking services to accommodate seasonal changes is essential for ensuring the well-being and safety of the dogs in your care. This chapter explores strategies for adjusting services across different seasons, managing extreme weather conditions, and maintaining dogs' safety in varying climates to provide optimal care year-round.

Adjusting Your Services for Different Seasons

Each season presents unique challenges and opportunities for dog walking professionals. Adjusting your services according to seasonal variations enhances comfort, safety, and enjoyment for dogs during walks:

Spring:

- **Temperature Management:** Monitor fluctuating temperatures and weather patterns. Adjust walking times to avoid peak heat or rain showers. Provide dogs with access to shaded areas and fresh water during breaks.
- **Allergen Awareness:** Be mindful of seasonal allergies affecting dogs. Watch for signs of discomfort or respiratory issues. Avoid walking in areas with high pollen counts or allergen exposure.
- **Paw Protection:** Check dogs' paw pads for sensitivity or irritation due to wet ground or allergens. Consider using protective paw balm or booties to prevent abrasions and maintain paw health.

Summer:

- **Heat Safety:** Prevent heat-related illnesses by scheduling walks during cooler times of the day, such as early morning or late

evening. Avoid hot pavement that can burn paws. Provide dogs with access to shaded areas, water breaks, and cooling measures (e.g., wet towels or cooling vests).
- **Hydration:** Ensure dogs stay hydrated during walks. Carry portable water bowls and offer water frequently. Monitor signs of dehydration, such as excessive panting or lethargy, and respond promptly.
- **Sun Protection:** Protect dogs from sun exposure and UV rays. Use pet-safe sunscreen on exposed areas, such as noses and ears, particularly for dogs with short coats or light-colored fur.

Fall:

- **Weather Changes:** Prepare for cooler temperatures and potential rainfall. Dress dogs in weather-appropriate gear, such as raincoats or sweaters, to maintain comfort during walks. Watch for slippery surfaces and fallen debris that may pose hazards.
- **Daylight Hours:** Adjust walking schedules as daylight hours shorten. Use reflective gear or LED collars for visibility during early morning or evening walks. Plan routes in well-lit areas to enhance safety.
- **Outdoor Safety:** Be mindful of seasonal activities, such as hunting or harvest activities, that may affect walking areas. Avoid areas with potential hazards, such as pesticides or wildlife, to minimize risks during walks.

Winter:

- **Cold Weather Precautions:** Protect dogs from cold temperatures, icy conditions, and wind chill. Dress dogs in insulated coats or sweaters. Limit exposure to freezing temperatures and use pet-safe de-icing products on sidewalks.
- **Paw Care:** Check dogs' paws for ice accumulation, cracks, or frostbite. Use paw balm to protect paw pads from salt or chemical exposure. Consider using booties to provide additional insulation and traction on icy surfaces.

- **Indoor Activities:** Offer indoor play sessions or enrichment activities on cold or snowy days. Maintain exercise routines with indoor games, mental stimulation toys, or interactive training sessions to keep dogs active and engaged.

Handling Extreme Weather Conditions

Navigating extreme weather conditions requires proactive measures to ensure dogs' safety and well-being during walks:

Heatwaves:

- **Early Morning or Late Evening Walks:** Schedule walks during cooler times of the day to avoid peak heat. Adjust walking intensity and duration based on temperature forecasts.
- **Hydration and Cooling:** Carry extra water and offer frequent water breaks. Use cooling vests, wet towels, or portable misters to lower body temperature gradually.
- **Signs of Heat Stress:** Monitor dogs for signs of heat exhaustion, including excessive panting, drooling, weakness, or collapse. Move dogs to shaded areas, provide water, and seek veterinary care if symptoms persist.

Thunderstorms:

- **Safety Shelter:** Plan alternative routes or seek shelter during thunderstorms to avoid lightning strikes or sudden weather changes. Monitor weather alerts and adjust walking schedules accordingly.
- **Comforting Dogs:** Comfort anxious dogs with calming techniques, such as gentle petting or providing a safe indoor environment. Use noise-reducing techniques, such as background music or white noise, to minimize anxiety during storms.

Snowstorms:

- **Visibility and Traction:** Enhance visibility with reflective gear or LED collars during snowy conditions. Use traction aids, such as booties or non-slip shoes, to prevent slipping on icy surfaces.
- **Paw Protection:** Check dogs' paws for ice accumulation and signs of frostbite. Use pet-safe de-icing products on sidewalks and wipe paws after walks to remove ice or salt residues.

Keeping Dogs Safe in Varying Climates

Adapting to diverse climates ensures dogs' safety and comfort across different geographic regions or seasonal changes:

Humid Climates:

- **Hydration:** Combat humidity-related dehydration by offering water breaks during walks. Monitor dogs for signs of heat exhaustion or fatigue.
- **Cooling Measures:** Use cooling vests, shade, or air-conditioned indoor breaks to prevent heat-related illnesses in humid climates.

Dry Climates:

- **Hydration:** Encourage water intake before and after walks to maintain hydration levels in dry climates. Provide portable water bowls and seek shaded areas during walks.
- **Paw Care:** Protect paw pads from hot pavement or rough terrain with booties or paw balm. Monitor signs of dryness or cracking due to low humidity levels.

Coastal Climates:

- **Beach Safety:** Monitor tidal changes and water conditions during beach walks. Prevent saltwater ingestion and rinse dogs with fresh water to remove sand or salt residues.

- **Sun Protection:** Use pet-safe sunscreen on exposed areas and offer shaded breaks during walks to prevent sunburn or heat exhaustion in coastal areas.

Conclusion

Adapting your dog walking services to seasonal variations and varying climates requires proactive planning, flexibility, and a commitment to maintaining dogs' safety and well-being. By adjusting service routines, monitoring weather conditions, and implementing safety precautions, you can enhance the quality of care, promote client satisfaction, and ensure enjoyable walking experiences year-round. Prioritize dogs' comfort, hydration, and protection from extreme weather elements to uphold professional standards and build trust with clients. By integrating seasonal considerations into your service approach, you can optimize pet care practices, mitigate weather-related risks, and cultivate a positive reputation as a reliable and compassionate dog walking professional in your community.

Chapter 26: Self-Care and Avoiding Burnout

Maintaining your well-being as a dog walking professional is crucial for sustaining your passion, energy, and effectiveness in the role. This chapter explores essential strategies for managing physical health, achieving work-life balance, and preventing burnout in a physically demanding job.

Managing Your Physical Health

As a dog walker, prioritizing your physical health ensures you can provide optimal care for the dogs under your supervision:

Physical Fitness: Incorporate regular exercise routines, such as walking, jogging, or strength training, to build endurance, improve stamina, and enhance overall fitness levels. Engage in activities that strengthen core muscles, promote flexibility, and support physical resilience during daily walks.

Proper Nutrition: Maintain a balanced diet rich in nutrients, vitamins, and hydration to sustain energy levels and support physical performance. Incorporate fresh fruits, vegetables, lean proteins, and whole grains into meals to fuel your body for demanding workdays.

Hydration: Drink an adequate amount of water throughout the day to prevent dehydration, maintain cognitive function, and support physical recovery. Carry a reusable water bottle during walks and prioritize hydration breaks to replenish fluids lost through exertion.

Posture and Ergonomics: Practice proper posture and ergonomic techniques to minimize strain on muscles, joints, and spinal alignment during prolonged walking sessions. Use supportive footwear, adjust carrying equipment for even weight distribution, and take periodic stretching breaks to alleviate tension and maintain mobility.

Finding Work-Life Balance

Achieving work-life balance is essential for nurturing personal well-being and preventing professional burnout:

Establishing Boundaries: Set clear boundaries between work and personal life to prioritize self-care, relaxation, and quality time with loved ones. Define dedicated work hours, schedule breaks between appointments, and resist the urge to overextend yourself beyond manageable limits.

Time Management: Implement effective time management strategies, such as prioritizing tasks, delegating responsibilities when feasible, and optimizing scheduling software to streamline administrative tasks. Allocate time for self-care activities, hobbies, and leisure pursuits to recharge and rejuvenate outside of work commitments.

Stress Management: Adopt stress management techniques, including deep breathing exercises, mindfulness meditation, or engaging in recreational activities that promote relaxation and mental clarity. Identify stress triggers, address underlying concerns proactively, and seek emotional support from peers or professional networks.

Social Support: Cultivate meaningful relationships with colleagues, friends, or mentors who understand the demands of your profession and provide encouragement, guidance, and perspective during challenging times. Share experiences, seek advice, and foster camaraderie within the pet care community to enhance emotional resilience and job satisfaction.

Avoiding Burnout in a Physically Demanding Job

Preventing burnout requires proactive strategies to preserve mental, emotional, and physical well-being over time:

Self-Assessment: Monitor signs of burnout, such as fatigue, irritability, diminished motivation, or physical discomfort, and acknowledge when additional support or adjustments are needed to restore balance. Prioritize self-awareness and listen to your body's signals to prevent prolonged stress or exhaustion.

Workload Management: Evaluate workload capacity and adjust client bookings, service offerings, or daily schedules to maintain sustainable work levels. Avoid overcommitting to appointments, negotiate realistic deadlines, and communicate boundaries effectively with clients to uphold service standards without compromising personal health.

Professional Development: Invest in continuous learning, skill development, or certification programs to expand expertise, enhance job satisfaction, and explore new opportunities within the pet care industry. Pursue professional interests, attend workshops or seminars, and stay informed about industry trends to remain engaged and inspired in your role.

Rest and Recovery: Prioritize adequate rest, sleep hygiene, and downtime to promote physical recovery, mental clarity, and emotional resilience. Incorporate relaxation techniques, such as progressive muscle relaxation or aromatherapy, into daily routines to alleviate tension and promote restorative sleep patterns.

Conclusion

Prioritizing self-care, maintaining work-life balance, and preventing burnout are essential for sustaining your well-being and professional efficacy as a dog walking professional. By integrating physical health practices, establishing boundaries, and cultivating resilience, you can navigate the demands of a physically demanding job with confidence and vitality. Embrace self-care as a cornerstone of your career longevity, nurture supportive relationships, and leverage stress management techniques to foster personal fulfillment and job satisfaction. By investing in your well-being, fostering work-life harmony, and implementing proactive strategies to prevent burnout, you can sustain passion, resilience, and professionalism in providing exceptional care for dogs and fostering positive client relationships in your dog walking business.

Chapter 27: Continuing Education and Certification

Continuing education and certification play pivotal roles in enhancing your expertise, credibility, and career advancement as a dog walking professional. This chapter explores the significance of ongoing learning, certification programs tailored for dog walkers, and strategies for staying abreast of evolving industry trends to maintain a competitive edge.

Importance of Ongoing Learning

Committing to lifelong learning fosters professional growth, expands your knowledge base, and equips you with updated skills and best practices:

Industry Evolution: The field of dog walking is dynamic, with advancements in animal behavior, safety protocols, and pet care technologies continually emerging. Embrace ongoing learning to adapt to industry changes, refine service offerings, and meet evolving client expectations effectively.

Enhanced Expertise: Engaging in continuing education opportunities, such as workshops, seminars, or online courses, deepens your understanding of canine behavior, health management, and handling techniques. Acquire specialized knowledge in areas like first aid, nutrition, or behavior modification to deliver comprehensive care and personalized solutions for dogs under your supervision.

Professional Development: Pursuing educational endeavors demonstrates your commitment to professional development and elevates your credibility as a knowledgeable and skilled dog walking professional. Stay informed about industry standards, ethical guidelines, and legal considerations to uphold integrity, professionalism, and client trust in your practice.

Certification Programs for Dog Walkers

Obtaining formal certification enhances your credentials, validates your expertise, and distinguishes you as a competent and qualified dog walking professional:

Certification Benefits: Enroll in accredited certification programs tailored for dog walkers to acquire specialized training, practical skills assessment, and recognition of competency in pet care practices. Certification validates your knowledge of safety protocols, animal welfare standards, and effective communication techniques essential for delivering quality service.

Skill Validation: Certification programs assess your proficiency in handling dogs, managing behavioral challenges, and implementing emergency response procedures. Gain hands-on experience, receive constructive feedback from industry experts, and refine your skills to enhance service delivery and client satisfaction.

Client Assurance: Certified dog walkers instill confidence in clients seeking reputable pet care providers committed to ethical standards, safety practices, and compassionate handling of animals. Display your certification credentials proudly to demonstrate professionalism, credibility, and dedication to delivering exceptional care for clients' beloved pets.

Staying Updated on Industry Trends

Remaining current with industry trends and innovations empowers you to adapt to market demands, capitalize on emerging opportunities, and maintain a competitive edge:

Industry Research: Monitor industry publications, pet care forums, and professional associations to stay informed about industry trends, regulatory changes, and technological advancements shaping the dog walking profession. Attend conferences, webinars, or networking events to engage with industry leaders, exchange insights, and explore innovative practices influencing pet care services.

Technological Integration: Embrace digital tools, such as scheduling software, GPS tracking systems, or online client portals, to streamline operations, enhance service efficiency, and improve communication with clients. Incorporate technology-driven solutions to optimize service delivery, track performance metrics, and adapt business strategies based on real-time data insights.

Client Expectations: Anticipate client preferences, preferences, and evolving pet care needs through proactive market research, client feedback analysis, and trend forecasting. Tailor service offerings, promotional campaigns, and customer engagement initiatives to align with current consumer trends, enhance client satisfaction, and foster long-term loyalty.

Conclusion

Continuing education, certification attainment, and industry trend awareness are integral components of professional development and career advancement in the dog walking industry. By embracing lifelong learning, pursuing certification programs, and staying abreast of evolving industry trends, you can elevate your expertise, enhance service quality, and cultivate a reputation as a trusted and knowledgeable pet care provider. Invest in your professional growth, expand your skill set, and leverage educational opportunities to remain competitive, resilient, and responsive to the evolving needs of pet owners and their beloved dogs. By committing to ongoing learning, achieving certification credentials, and adapting to industry advancements, you can forge a successful career path as a respected dog walking professional dedicated to delivering exemplary care, promoting animal welfare, and fostering meaningful client relationships in your community.

Chapter 28: Case Studies and Success Stories

Exploring case studies and success stories from established dog walking businesses offers invaluable insights, practical tips, and inspirational examples to inform and inspire your own entrepreneurial journey. This chapter delves into real-life examples of thriving dog walking enterprises, highlighting their strategies, challenges overcome, and lessons learned that you can apply to elevate your business.

Learning from Successful Dog Walking Businesses

Studying successful dog walking businesses provides a blueprint for achieving sustainable growth, client satisfaction, and industry recognition:

Market Differentiation: Identify unique selling propositions (USPs) that distinguish leading dog walking businesses in your area. Analyze their service offerings, customer experience strategies, and brand positioning to uncover effective approaches for attracting and retaining clients.

Operational Excellence: Evaluate operational efficiencies, scheduling systems, and client communication protocols implemented by successful businesses. Adopt best practices in service delivery, time management, and resource allocation to streamline workflows, optimize productivity, and enhance service consistency.

Client-Centric Approach: Examine strategies for building strong client relationships, understanding pet owner preferences, and addressing individualized pet care needs. Implement personalized service offerings, responsive communication channels, and proactive client engagement initiatives to foster loyalty and trust among your clientele.

Real-Life Examples and Tips

Explore compelling case studies and actionable tips from thriving dog walking businesses that have achieved notable success in the industry:

Case Study 1: Pawsitive Trails Dog Walking

- **Business Strategy:** Pawsitive Trails differentiated itself by specializing in off-leash adventure hikes for dogs, emphasizing personalized attention and small group sizes.
- **Key Success Factor:** Establishing trust through transparent communication, comprehensive safety protocols, and certified pet first aid training for staff members.
- **Tip:** Offer unique service experiences, such as nature hikes or specialized training sessions, to cater to adventurous pet owners seeking enriching activities for their dogs.

Case Study 2: Urban Paws Pet Services

- **Business Strategy:** Urban Paws integrated technology-driven solutions, including GPS tracking for real-time pet monitoring and online scheduling platforms for seamless client bookings.
- **Key Success Factor:** Leveraging social media platforms to showcase client testimonials, educational content on pet care, and behind-the-scenes glimpses of daily operations.
- **Tip:** Harness the power of social media marketing to enhance brand visibility, engage with target audiences, and cultivate a community of loyal pet owners and advocates.

Case Study 3: Happy Tails Dog Walking

- **Business Strategy:** Happy Tails prioritized continuous staff training, including behavioral management techniques and ongoing professional development in pet care best practices.
- **Key Success Factor:** Building a reputation for reliability, consistency, and exceptional customer service through personalized pet care plans and responsive client communication.
- **Tip:** Invest in staff training programs, certifications, and skill development to ensure high-quality service delivery, client satisfaction, and business growth.

Applying Their Strategies to Your Business

Integrate insights gleaned from successful dog walking businesses into your own entrepreneurial endeavors to achieve measurable results and sustainable growth:

Strategic Planning: Develop a comprehensive business plan aligned with identified market opportunities, competitive analysis, and client demographics. Define clear goals, performance metrics, and actionable strategies for achieving long-term success in the dog walking industry.

Client Engagement: Implement proactive client engagement strategies, such as personalized service offerings, client feedback surveys, and loyalty rewards programs, to enhance satisfaction, retention rates, and referral business.

Innovation and Adaptation: Embrace innovation by adopting technological advancements, industry trends, and emerging pet care solutions to optimize service efficiency, operational agility, and competitive advantage in a dynamic marketplace.

Conclusion

Exploring case studies and success stories from leading dog walking businesses provides valuable lessons, actionable insights, and inspiration for aspiring entrepreneurs in the pet care industry. By studying market leaders, analyzing their business strategies, and applying proven tactics to your own operations, you can cultivate a distinctive brand identity, foster client trust, and achieve sustainable growth. Embrace continuous learning, adapt to evolving industry trends, and prioritize client satisfaction to establish a reputation as a trusted and reputable dog walking professional in your community. By leveraging real-life examples, implementing best practices, and refining your business approach, you can navigate challenges, seize opportunities, and position your dog walking business for long-term success and prosperity in the competitive pet care landscape.

Chapter 29: Handling Business Challenges

Navigating challenges is an inevitable part of running a dog walking business. This chapter explores common obstacles in the industry, effective problem-solving techniques, and strategies for maintaining motivation during tough times to foster resilience and long-term success.

Common Challenges in the Dog Walking Industry

Understanding the challenges unique to the dog walking industry equips you with foresight and preparedness to address potential hurdles effectively:

Client Retention: Retaining clients amidst competitive market dynamics and fluctuating demand requires consistent service excellence, proactive communication, and personalized client engagement strategies.

Seasonal Variability: Adapting services to seasonal changes, extreme weather conditions, and fluctuating demand for pet care services presents operational challenges and requires flexible scheduling and contingency planning.

Staffing and Training: Recruiting reliable staff, ensuring adherence to safety protocols, and maintaining consistent service quality across team members pose staffing challenges that impact business operations and client satisfaction.

Regulatory Compliance: Navigating local regulations, obtaining necessary permits, and ensuring legal compliance in pet care operations requires meticulous attention to regulatory requirements and proactive engagement with local authorities.

Problem-Solving Techniques

Effective problem-solving techniques empower you to address challenges proactively, mitigate risks, and foster operational resilience:

Root Cause Analysis: Identify underlying factors contributing to business challenges through systematic evaluation, data analysis, and stakeholder input to develop targeted solutions and preventive measures.

Collaborative Approach: Foster collaboration with team members, industry peers, and business mentors to leverage collective expertise, brainstorm innovative solutions, and gain diverse perspectives on overcoming challenges.

Adaptability and Flexibility: Embrace adaptability in response to changing market conditions, client preferences, and industry trends by adjusting business strategies, service offerings, and operational processes accordingly.

Continuous Improvement: Implement a culture of continuous improvement through feedback loops, performance metrics, and ongoing evaluation of business practices to enhance efficiency, service quality, and client satisfaction.

Staying Motivated During Tough Times

Maintaining motivation during challenging periods is essential for sustaining enthusiasm, resilience, and commitment to your dog walking business:

Goal Setting: Set achievable short-term and long-term goals aligned with business objectives, personal aspirations, and professional growth to maintain focus, track progress, and celebrate milestones.

Self-Care Practices: Prioritize self-care routines, including exercise, relaxation techniques, and time spent outdoors, to recharge mentally, physically, and emotionally amidst the demands of running a dog walking business.

Positive Mindset: Cultivate a positive mindset through mindfulness practices, gratitude exercises, and affirming self-talk to foster resilience, navigate setbacks, and maintain optimism during challenging times.

Support Network: Seek support from friends, family members, and fellow entrepreneurs within the pet care community to share experiences, seek guidance, and receive encouragement during periods of uncertainty or adversity.

Conclusion

Embracing challenges as opportunities for growth, learning, and innovation positions you to navigate obstacles effectively, strengthen business resilience, and achieve sustainable success in the competitive dog walking industry. By understanding common challenges, applying proactive problem-solving techniques, and prioritizing self-motivation and resilience, you can overcome adversity, optimize business operations, and cultivate a rewarding career as a trusted pet care provider. Embrace a proactive approach to addressing challenges, foster a supportive network of peers, and prioritize personal well-being to sustain enthusiasm, perseverance, and professional excellence in your journey as a dog walking business owner. By embracing challenges as opportunities for growth, learning, and innovation, you can navigate obstacles effectively, strengthen business resilience, and achieve sustainable success in the competitive dog walking industry

Chapter 30: Future Trends in the Dog Walking Industry

Anticipating and adapting to future trends in the dog walking industry is essential for staying competitive, meeting evolving client expectations, and positioning your business for long-term success. This chapter explores emerging trends, technological advancements, and strategic planning considerations to navigate changes in the market and cultivate a thriving future for your dog walking business.

Emerging Trends and Technologies

Staying informed about emerging trends and technological innovations enables you to capitalize on opportunities and meet evolving client needs effectively:

Technology Integration: Embrace digital solutions, such as GPS tracking systems, mobile apps for client communication, and automated scheduling platforms, to enhance service efficiency, streamline operations, and optimize client experience.

Health and Wellness Services: Expand service offerings to include holistic pet care solutions, such as nutritional counseling, specialized exercise programs, and wellness check-ups, to address growing demand for comprehensive pet health management.

Environmental Sustainability: Adopt eco-friendly practices, such as biodegradable waste bags, carbon-neutral transportation options, and sustainable business operations, to appeal to environmentally conscious clients and support corporate social responsibility initiatives.

Personalized Service Experiences: Customize service packages, offer personalized pet care plans, and incorporate client feedback mechanisms to deliver tailored experiences that prioritize individual pet preferences, behavior profiles, and health requirements.

Adapting to Changes in the Market

Proactively adapting to market changes ensures business resilience, agility, and responsiveness to shifting consumer preferences and industry dynamics:

Market Research: Conduct regular market research, client surveys, and competitor analysis to monitor industry trends, identify emerging opportunities, and anticipate consumer behavior shifts that impact pet care service demand.

Diversified Service Offerings: Expand service repertoire to include additional pet care services, such as pet sitting, grooming, or specialized training programs, to diversify revenue streams, attract new clientele, and enhance business scalability.

Client Engagement Strategies: Enhance client engagement through personalized communication channels, interactive client portals, and educational content on pet care best practices to build trust, foster loyalty, and cultivate long-term client relationships.

Agile Business Practices: Implement agile business practices, flexible service delivery models, and adaptive operational strategies to pivot swiftly in response to market fluctuations, seasonal demand variations, and unforeseen economic challenges.

Planning for the Future of Your Business

Strategic planning considerations enable you to envision growth opportunities, set ambitious goals, and proactively shape the future trajectory of your dog walking business:

Goal Setting: Define clear short-term and long-term goals aligned with business objectives, financial milestones, and personal aspirations to guide strategic decision-making, measure progress, and celebrate achievements.

Professional Development: Invest in ongoing education, certification programs, and skill enhancement initiatives to stay abreast of industry trends, cultivate specialized expertise, and maintain competitive advantage in the evolving pet care landscape.

Financial Management: Prioritize financial stability, budgeting, and cash flow management to sustain business operations, fund growth initiatives, and withstand economic fluctuations while maintaining profitability and fiscal responsibility.

Community Engagement: Establish community partnerships, sponsor local pet events, and engage in charitable initiatives to enhance brand visibility, foster community goodwill, and cultivate a loyal customer base invested in supporting your business's success.

Conclusion

By embracing future trends, adapting to market changes, and planning strategically, you can position your dog walking business for sustained growth, client satisfaction, and industry leadership in the dynamic pet care sector. Anticipate emerging trends, leverage technological innovations, and prioritize client-centric service delivery to differentiate your business, inspire customer loyalty, and achieve long-term success as a trusted provider of quality pet care services. Embrace innovation, agility, and forward-thinking strategies to navigate industry evolution, capitalize on growth opportunities, and shape a prosperous future for your dog walking business in an ever-changing marketplace.

Conclusion: Embracing Your Journey in the Dog Walking Business

Congratulations on reaching the conclusion of this comprehensive guide to starting and succeeding in the dog walking business. Throughout this book, we've explored every facet of launching, managing, and growing your own venture in the vibrant pet care industry. From understanding the fundamentals of dog behavior to navigating legal requirements, setting up your business, and mastering client relationships, you've gained invaluable insights and practical strategies to embark on this rewarding entrepreneurial journey.

As you venture into the world of dog walking, remember that your passion for animals, dedication to exceptional service, and commitment to continuous learning will be your greatest assets. Embrace challenges as opportunities for growth, innovate with technological advancements, and adapt to evolving market trends to stay ahead in this dynamic field.

Always prioritize the well-being of the dogs in your care, nurture strong client relationships, and maintain the highest standards of professionalism. Your reputation as a trusted pet care provider will flourish as you deliver on your promises and exceed expectations.

As you move forward, envision your future with optimism and determination. Set ambitious goals, celebrate milestones, and never stop learning and evolving. Whether you're just starting out or expanding your services, each step you take brings you closer to realizing your vision for a successful and fulfilling dog walking business.

With all my best wishes for your success,